Start Your Own

FLORIST SHOP AND OTHER FLORAL BUSINESSES

Additional titles in *Entrepreneur's **Startup Series***

Start Your Own

Entrepreneur.
MAGAZINE'S

start*up*

Start Your Own

FLORIST SHOP AND OTHER FLORAL BUSINESSES

Your Step-by-Step
Guide to Success

Entrepreneur Press and Cheryl Kimball

EP
Entrepreneur.
Press

Editorial Director: Jere L. Calmes
Managing Editor: Marla Markman
Cover Design: Beth Hansen-Winter
Production: Eliot House Productions
Composition: Patricia Miller

This publication is designed to provide accurate and authoritative information in regard to the subject matter covered. It is sold with the understanding that the publisher is not engaged in rendering legal, accounting or other professional services. If legal advice or other expert assistance is required, the services of a competent professional person should be sought.

Library of Congress Cataloging-in-Publication Data
Kimball, Cheryl.
    Start your own florist shop and other floral businesses/by Entrepreneur Press and Cheryl Kimball.
        p.   cm.
    Includes index.
    ISBN-13: 978-1-59918-027-4 (alk. paper)
    ISBN-10: 1-59918-027-8 (alk. paper)
        1. Florists. 2. New business enterprises—Management. I. Entrepreneur Press. II. Title.
    SB443.K56 2006
    745.92068'1—dc22   2006004273

Printed in Canada

12 11 10 09 08 07 06   10 9 8 7 6 5 4 3 2 1

Contents

Chapter 5

The Business Side of Flowers **33**

Chapter 6

Insurance and Legal Matters **47**

Chapter 7

Outfitting a Flower Shop. **55**

Chapter 8

Flowers, Flowers, Wherefore Art Thou?. 63

Chapter 9

Helpful Professional Credentials and Training 71

Preface

What a lovely business to be in, surrounding yourself with beautiful flowers every day. But before you get too caught up in smelling the roses, you should spend some time with this book. The florist business can be lucrative and gratifying, but like any business, knowledge and planning are the keys to success.

Just because you are in the business of posies doesn't mean you don't need accounting services—you do! Building maintenance, delivery service, and other mundane topics need to be familiar to you. And a thorough understanding of

▲

customer service is key in this business. For instance, depending on the kind of floral business you start, you are often dealing with grieving people ordering funeral flowers. And your busiest seasons are ones of high stress, like Christmas and Easter, and your customers will expect perfection.

But if you head into this business with all the tools you need for that basic business framework, you can relax and get involved in the real heart of the floral industry—creativity and beauty!

She Loves Me,
She Loves Me Not
Is the Floral Business
Right for You?

You doodle with a garden every year, growing some vegetables, but you like to grow flowers the most. You always give flowers as gifts, and you never leave the grocery store without a bouquet—or two—for yourself. You even took a floral arrangement class a couple years ago just for the fun of it. But does that make starting a florist business perfect for you? Maybe, but not necessarily. There are a lot of things to consider before you open up shop.

To be a florist it certainly is an advantage to love flowers. But talk to any small business owner, and a theme you hear repeatedly is that the surprising part of any business is all the things you spend your time on that have nothing to do with your core focus. A friend recently said after buying three bouquets at the grocery store, "I always thought being a florist would be a great job. What could make you more happy than being surrounded by beautiful flowers?" But no matter what you sell, you need to focus on some accounting, some building maintenance, perhaps some collections, and usually a whole lot of customer service.

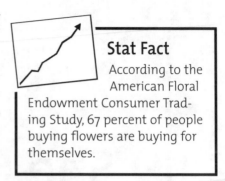

Stat Fact
According to the American Floral Endowment Consumer Trading Study, 67 percent of people buying flowers are buying for themselves.

Terry L. of Strafford, New Hampshire, came by her florist interests genetically— her grandmother had a florist shop on Main Street in a small New Hampshire city. Terry spent lots of time as a child in her grandmother's shop. She learned to arrange flowers. And she also saw firsthand how much of the florist business is about customer service. "There is a lot more to [being a florist] than people think there is," Terry says. "You really have to know how to work with customers." And, she adds, you are typically working with people during the most stressful events of their lives, namely weddings and funerals.

The best part of being a florist is how special your creations make people feel. But that is just one of the many things to consider when you are thinking about starting your own floral business.

Where to Start

No matter what business you start, there are some basic steps that you will need to take. They include

- determining what you want out of your business, both financially and professionally,
- determining if there is a market for a floral business in your area,
- choosing an organizational structure,
- creating a business plan,
- getting financing if necessary,
- obtaining the required licenses and permits,
- getting any education you need to learn more about the floral business,
- setting up your base of operations, and

- creating marketing materials to attract customers.

The floral industry is so diverse that you can set up in your own home (provided the zoning in your neighborhood allows home businesses), in the back corner of a large warehouse, or a retail location on a busy main street.

The choice to have a retail florist shop is perhaps your most important financial decision because rent or a mortgage is expensive. And you will need to make the storefront and the shop very attractive to passersby. However, no matter what you choose, there isn't too much costly overhead, that is, equipment to buy.

Are You and Flowers a Match?

I'll get to the nitty gritty business stuff in a while, but the very first thing you need to think about is whether flowers and you are a match. What do you want out of your business? Some potential business owners don't care what their specific businesses are as long as the financial potential is in line with their entrepreneurial vision. Others target an industry—like flowers—and tailor their interest by which end of the business (retail or wholesale) they choose to get into.

Some people forget to consider the fundamental aspects of a particular industry. In the case of flowers, something to consider is whether you have the personal constitution to deal with having a main product that is perishable. Would knowing that the cooler full of roses is going bad keep you awake at night? Are you organized enough to order as close to on-demand as possible to avoid as much of this spoilage as you can?

And, don't forget, operating a retail store or a wholesale business is a very challenging world. Consider how you like to spend your day. So before you even sniff a single rose, you need to figure out what part of the florist industry is right for you.

Retail Flowers

Wherever you choose to locate your retail florist shop—Main Street, a strip mall, or even at the hospital—you will come up against many of the same retail space considerations. After location, which is covered in greater detail in Chapter 3, there are lots of things unique to the

> **Bright Idea**
>
> It's always a good idea to have worked for someone else for a time in the type of business you are considering opening. Don't be sneaky about your intentions; look for a job at a location that won't compete with your eventual start-up, and let the proprietor know your plans. People are often thrilled to hire someone who is serious about learning the business, and you may ultimately be able to work together on some things.

retail scenario that you need to consider when deciding whether this side of the floral business is right for you.

A main consideration is you have to be there! Your shop will need regular hours; the hours will need to suit your potential customers, and you will need to be in the shop during those hours. That's right—until you can afford employees, the person in the shop will be you. And even if you do have an employee, customers expect to see the proprietor at least some of the time, especially if you are the florist. (There is also the option of hiring professional floral designers and florists, either as employees or independent contractors.) Customers will expect you to be there, perhaps creating their floral arrangements, but at the least, listening carefully to what they want you to create.

So, in a retail business, you will potentially spend a lot of time in the shop. Unless you start out extremely well funded, you will be doing most of the retail work yourself. Perhaps you can hire someone to be in the shop for you, but having more than one or two part-time employees is a hard pill for a start-up business proprietor to swallow. If you are good at designing floral arrangements, you don't want to be driving the delivery truck while someone less talented is back at the shop making the creations your customers are buying. And besides, it's unlikely you chose the floral business so you could drive a truck.

You will want to be at the shop and let someone else do the deliveries. This means you either have to be able to afford two employees—one to do deliveries and one to take care of customers while you are arranging flowers—or have your shop set up so that you can arrange flowers in a place where you can greet customers, too. That, in turn, will take away from the time you are able to devote to creating memorable arrangements that will put your stamp on the market and bring repeat business. Ah, the compromises!

The bottom line is: Can you do retail? Is your idea of a good work life standing in a retail shop greeting customers? Is being confined to a retail shop something you can handle? Chances are your start-up retail shop will probably be rather small: Will you have a problem not only being confined but also being confined to a small space? Many owners of retail start-ups talk about working 60 to 80 hours a week for the first year of business. Although this isn't recommended because it can quickly lead to burnout, you can expect to spend most weeks working well beyond the traditional 40.

Your hope with any business is to have repeat customers. With a retail storefront, you often come face-to-face with your customers—the ones you like and the ones that aren't so pleasant. Is that kind of customer service something you can deal with? Can you smile and disarm the cranky customer? Do you have the personality to deal with face-to-face interactions that may include having your creations

Fun Fact

In 2001, 26,200 retail florists averaged $250,191 in annual sales.

criticized? Of course, it's important to remember that you will also—and probably more often than not or you won't be in business long—be praised for your creations and your service. That is something most anyone can take, face-to-face, over the phone, or however!

Wholesale Florist Service

The wholesale florist business is a different story all together. This doesn't tend to be a start-up kind of business, but if retail doesn't appeal to you and you really want to be in the floral industry, then perhaps wholesale is right for you.

You still have customers, but they are businesses, not individuals. Just don't believe for one minute that business owners make customer service easier than individual customers! They often can be even more tricky because their business success depends in part upon the quality of your service and the products they get from you.

Wholesaling flowers can take a couple angles: One is the wholesaler who supplies direct to the industry—they are unloading shipments of flowers from the growers, often exported from foreign markets, and selling them in bulk at wholesale prices. The other is the middle wholesaler who takes orders from local flower shops, goes to the major wholesalers' market (typically at around three in the morning), makes the purchases, and brings them back for the local florists to pick up. The individual florists can buy at the market themselves, too, but like all things, the best prices go to the bulk purchasers. So you often don't save much money. And you have to be at the market in the wee hours of the morning, which is not conducive to then spending the day in the retail shop.

If you choose the wholesale end of the industry, you will spend a lot of time with the raw materials. Depending on what your role is, you may rarely even see an actual flower. Again, like the delivery vehicle, it is doubtful you will have chosen to get into the floral business to load cardboard boxes and drive refrigerated trucks around, so perhaps you will actually be at the flower markets making purchases, deciding which flowers are the freshest, and filling orders for your retail customers. Sound like fun? It is, except don't forget the wee hours of the morning part. Deliveries of fresh goods need to make it to the retail stores to fill yesterdays special orders and before their customers begin calling in orders.

Again, how do you want to spend your day?

Fun Fact

Seventy-two percent of the flowers sold that are grown in the United States are grown in the state of California. But 70 percent of all fresh flowers sold in the United States are imported from other countries. By far the top grower is Columbia, with Ecuador, the European Union, Canada, Costa Rica, and Mexico falling behind Columbia. (Statistics from the Society of American Florists)

Wholesale Supplies

The other type of wholesaling involves providing florists with the supplies they need to create their arrangements: wire, vases, ribbons, florist's paper, notecards, foam, and preservatives all need to come from somewhere. Although in a pinch, florists can run to their local craft suppliers or drugstores to pick up one or two items, this is not the way to make money. The supplies that florists use on a regular basis need to be bought as cheaply as possible in the largest quantities that make sense for the size of the business.

To do this supplying, you would need to have a warehouse space of some sort to store the supplies—is taking on that kind of real estate something you had in mind? You could start in your garage, but to give florists the prices they need in order to be able to mark things up enough to make money, you need to be able to stock enough bulk to make your own purchase price as low as possible. So your garage isn't going to cut it for long. The storage space also needs to be accessible for large delivery trucks and for florists who pick up their supplies.

Is hanging out in a warehouse your idea of fun? Is handling the floral supplies but not the actual flowers the part of the industry you had in mind? It can be great fun to pick out unique supplies and to manage large inventory, but you need to think up front about the fact that the flowers themselves are a step away.

Smart Tip

Tip...

Even if you think it is going to be a few years before you open your own florist business, it is never too early to start getting experience. Keep your day job but find part-time work in a flower shop. You can earn a little extra money on the side doing something you enjoy while learning the ins and outs of the business.

The Greenhouse

A "greenhouse" usually refers to the part of the plant market that sells live plants, either for indoors or outdoors. What part of the country you are in will have a great impact on how this business is going to work for you. In the northern climates, you can probably expect to close up shop from Christmas until Easter if your business is mainly live outdoor plants. No matter how you structure the business, in the spring you will be extremely busy with homeowners and businesses and their landscapers purchasing the plants they need.

Things will slow down in summer although they can still be pretty busy with homeowners changing their landscape designs, new homes finishing construction, and people replacing plants that didn't make it or to reflect the season. You can supplement those slower times with additional inventory like seeds, pots, potting soil, and garden furniture. For Easter, you would, of course, stock a large inventory of lilies,

> **Beware!**
> If you tend to be sensitive to things, you will want to be careful about the use of pesticides on the plants that you work with. You could use this to your advantage and market yourself as a pesticide-free florist!

and around Thanksgiving start stocking poinsettias and holiday arrangements and perhaps even a little sideline of fresh trees and wreaths.

Although winter is down time for retail sales in cold climates, you will be busy looking through catalogs and creating orders for the next season's inventory, perhaps starting seeds for new plants, and cleaning and repairing the retail space. Or you may want to get these things done in the slower times during the selling season so you can be doing some other moneymaking venture (perhaps working in a similar operation in a warm location!) or taking courses to expand what you can offer. More temperate climates allow such operations to remain open year round, but there are still busier planting seasons and down times.

Cut Flower Garden, Farmer's Market, or Roadside Stand

Do you have the space to grow a lot of "cut flowers"? Cut flowers are those that are commonly used in bouquets. If you can grow a sufficient quantity of high enough quality, you can have a business selling your flowers to local florists. Another outlet is the increasingly popular farmer's market, which can simply be tables in the bank parking lot in town every Saturday morning or a purpose-built building in a busy location where "farmers" rent space to sell their wares.

If you have the space to grow the flowers and the location to put up your own roadside stand, you can stay at home and tend to your flowers and count on passersby to stop and purchase bouquets. This can work fine if you get traffic along your road. If you can afford to advertise a little, you can even pull in customers who don't travel your road but would make a short side trip to a destination point. And they can become regular customers.

> **Beware!**
> Think out of the box when it comes to deciding the kind of floral business that is right for you. You don't want to spend all the effort and money it costs to start a retail florist shop to find that after the newness wears off you cringe at the thought of spending another day locked in a shop.

For this, you would probably want to have other things for sale as well—perhaps handmade woolens or baskets or maple syrup that you also produce. This would make even more sense if the products can be produced in a season completely different from the main flower-growing season.

But again, you need to think carefully about your personal leanings—having a roadside stand at your place means that strangers will be on your property. You probably won't have enough customers to make it practical to spend all day in the stand, so you need to be okay about being interrupted—hopefully regularly if you have enough business.

Is There a Market?

One of the two most important aspects to any business start-up is how to get your market to know you exist (see Chapter 10). But even before you get to that point, you need to determine if there is in fact a market for the type of floral business you are considering in the area in which you are considering. Your market research is going to depend on what kind of floral business you want:

- Retail florist shop, including deliveries.
- Wholesale floral business, where retail florists come to you for their supplies.
- Full-scale greenhouse where you sell cut flower arrangements as well as live plants, maybe even to the point of being called a "nursery," which usually implies you grow the live plants as well.
- Farmer's market, pick-your-own, or at-the-source flower sales.

Once you decide the floral business you want, you need to determine where you might like to do that. Then, you can research whether the market is already covered in that area. Check the Yellow Pages, do an online search, and by all means drive around. Talk with the local funeral home and wedding planners to find out where their customersr make their flower purchases. Be sure to tell them you are thinking about starting a florist business.

If you are considering a wholesale operation, get a list of potential customers in the market range you plan to cover and start calling—would they purchase from you if you opened a wholesale floral supplies business? What kinds of things do they purchase? What do they find hard to get? What would they like to purchase? What services would they like you to provide?

> **Tip...**
>
> **Smart Tip**
> Terry L. reminds potential flower shop owners to be patient. If you do the best you can and follow some simple rules, "Everything comes in its time."

Once you determine that you could enjoy a certain type of florist business and there is a market you can service in a given area, it's time to think about setting up shop.

A Day in the Life
of a Florist

Where your shop is located and the type of customers in your area will have a great bearing on how your day is spent as the owner of a florist shop. Despite these general differences, there are a lot of things that are the same for every shop owner.

In the Beginning

There is, says Kristina, owner of An Array of Flowers & Gifts in southern New Hampshire, some routine like any other job. The first thing she does when she unlocks the door is make sure that the front of the shop is ready for customers. A very nice presentation is critical for sales and for repeat customers. The reach-in coolers are checked for how they look and whether they need restocking. Basically everything that the customer will see when he walks in is checked to be sure that what the customer sees is very appealing.

Customer Orders

Once the shop is ready for walk-in business, the next thing Kristina does is check the computer for orders that come in from FTD, Teleflora, and other floral wire services. Also, checking the phone messages for calls from customers who would like to place an order that day is critical. And lastly, there may be orders waiting in the wings that were placed a few days before for delivery today. These orders become the priority of what needs to be delivered later in the day. Some days there are lots of orders, says Kristina, and some days there are not.

Flower Orders

Next, you need to check your stock based on the orders that are waiting to be filled. Depending on the number and type of orders that await, you may need to order flowers. Some may need to be delivered later that day; some may just need to be ordered to fill stock that will be depleted once the current orders are filled.

Special Occasions

As much as a month ahead of time for significant flower holidays such as Valentine's Day, you need to start getting a handle on what you need in stock. Kristina makes calls to her vendors to check on what she ordered last year. She checks her books to see whether her sales are on the rise. Using those records, she makes decisions about how much stock to order and what other supplies she might need to be ready for the huge Valentine's rush.

Walk-Ins

Amidst all of this, customers may be coming and going. Kristina emphasizes that "customers always come first." An Array of Flowers is near a medium-sized hospital, a location that is conducive to walk-in business. You need to be prepared to drop everything and wait on the customers standing in front of you. While phone orders are crucial and deserve plenty of attention, if people have made the effort to get in the car and come to your shop, they should expect prompt excellent service.

Arranging

If you are a florist and do the arranging in your shop, you will be spending a lot of time behind the scenes filling the day's orders. And depending the size of your shop, you will probably have at least one employee to take care of the phone, the walk-in customers, order pick-ups, and orders ready to head out on the delivery van.

Deliveries

There are two kinds of deliveries you need to be keeping tabs on throughout the day: the ones coming in to stock your store and the ones that need to go out. Some shop owners do some portion of their own deliveries. Some use a delivery service. Some have their own delivery vans and hire retired moms or dads or teenage drivers to deliver after school. Deliveries need to get to their destinations at the times you promised. Your shop's reputation depends on it.

The deliveries from vendors will also interrupt your day. Flowers will typically be coming in every day. Some need more immediate attention than others, either because of their delicacy or because they are needed in an arrangement right away.

Behind the Scenes

As a shop owner, Kristina says you should be spend time on cost control. She has a business background and is very conscious of how much her stock costs. She shops around for the best price. If she can buy an order of lilies for $23 from one vendor and $17 from another, she tends toward the lower price. If the quality is significantly less, that is a matter for consideration. But it has to be $6 less. Most customers do not understand the difference between paying one amount or the other when it comes to the final price of the arrangement. Of course, you don't want the flowers wilting before they even leave the shop. It's all a balancing act.

Useful Traits

Mary B. of Wyoming Florists near Cincinnati points to the importance of being able to multitask. She also recommends hiring employees who are good at juggling many different things at once.

One of the most important traits that the front person in your shop needs is a positive relationship with customers. Without customers, the shop would not exist. And while you certainly don't need to cater to abusive customers, you do want to be able to fill customers' needs and desires as much as possible. As Mary B. says, "There are customers that are hard to deal with, and you are dealing with different personalities day in and day out." But the flip side, she says, is that "customers can also bring you out of the doldrums."

Ultimately, the business is one of diversity. Your location, how you set up your shop, and what floral niches you focus on will have a great bearing on the types of things you spend your day doing. But however you do it, you will be spending the day amidst the beauty of flowers!

The Main Types
of Floral
Businesses

s Chapter 1 pointed out, you can enter the
floral market in many ways. The three main ones are a retail
shop, a wholesaler selling flowers, or starting a wholesale floral
supplies outlet. What do you need to know to be successful in
each?

Retail

There was a time when almost every town's Main Street had a drugstore, a shoe repair shop, and a florist. Drugstores have mostly vanished to the edges of town, and shoe repair shops have disappeared almost entirely. Whether or not there is a florist is more hit or miss than it once was. But where there is one, it usually has been there for a long time.

So unless you are buying out a business, opening a retail florist on Main Street probably will entail competing with a well-established business. There is always the dream of inventing the better mousetrap. Competing successfully with any established business can certainly be accomplished, but expect to work hard and have some unique approach in order to do that. And, of course, Main Street itself will be perhaps the most expensive location, so you need to be sure there is a serious market for your retail shop.

These days, the best retail location for a flower business may be on the outskirts of town in a strip mall or other retail cluster. In town can offer a more upscale setting, but if you pick your mall location to match the type of store you want, you can certainly find an appropriate retail shop outside of town.

The nation's 22,753 retail florists average $290,000 annual sales per shop in 2005 (California Cut Flowers Statistics), much of which is via telephone. The phone-in business is enhanced by passersby. If they see your shop regularly as they travel from one place in town to another, they will be more likely to think of you when they need to order flowers.

Some questions to ask before setting up your business anywhere are:

- Is there a flower shop in town already?
- If so, is there enough of a market for two?
- If not, why not? Can that be changed? Is there something that makes the area not a good location for a flower shop?
- Is there a real advantage to being on Main Street as opposed to being in a less costly retail location?

Bright Idea

If you buy supplies in large quantities to take advantage of getting the lowest prices, consider renting a storage unit somewhere convenient between your store and home, probably closer to the former. You will want to be able to get to it easily and quickly. But if you store supplies off-site, be sure to keep good records of what is there. This is important not only for tax purposes but also so you can be sure not to order more of something you already have as well as know what you have in order to use it up. This is also a good place to store seasonal supplies. Keep things in the boxes they came in or invest in plastic storage bins to ensure that materials stay as fresh as when you first bought them.

- What locations are available? What shop space would you want if you could choose from any in town? Does the available space have at least a large percentage of these qualities?
- Can a delivery vehicle get in and out of the location easily? And, is there plenty of space for loading a van with arrangements?

Of course, the very first consideration is probably going to have to be the monthly rental cost of the location. If your ideal spot seems too expensive, don't give up until you know you are comparing apples and apples. For instance, what is included in the rent? Perhaps the space that seems too expensive comes with heat included, free parking, free trash pickup, or some other amenities that can make up in part for the additional monthly lease amount.

Ultimately, you need to be realistic about the amount of rent revenue you can afford. But there are some retail space features that any florist shop will need to have. Not the least of these is display space, including in-store display as well as window display. Refrigeration is a key item for flowers, which are considered perishables. You will need counter space to work on and storage space to keep the clutter of stored supplies out of sight. And amidst all of this, your shop will simply need space for customers to get around. Let's consider each of these more carefully.

Window Display

A window display area is almost a must for the flower shop. It doesn't have to be enormous but it needs to have enough space for you to create noticeable displays of your shop's arranging prowess. The window should preferably not be a southern exposure where floral displays would be subject to long hours of blistering hot sun. And it should be changed—often! Drooping, brown flowers and dusty vases are not the message you want to send to potential customers. And even if the display gets dusted and looks nice, a window display that has gone on too long begins to make people wonder if you are closed. Striking, season- or holiday-appropriate displays call attention to your shop and give customers and passersby reason to tell others about your business.

Refrigeration

Flowers need to be kept cool. Preferably, your shop should be able to accommodate a walk-in cooler—a floor-to-ceiling appliance that you can literally walk into. It needs to be located somewhere in the back, near where arrangements are

Tip...

Smart Tip
Encourage budding florists! Use up some of your aging flowers and teach a kids' flower arranging class. You could even offer to do it in the local school around a holiday and send each child home with a small arrangement with a card attached that has your business information on it.

put together and close to a back entrance where you can unload shipments of flowers. You will need room for a reach-in cooler on the retail sales floor space.

Both of these need an appropriate electrical supply, which you must work out with your landlord ahead of time. If the lease comes with electricity paid for, your landlord may want to add a surcharge for these electricity-hungry appliances. See Chapter 7 for more detailed discussion of refrigeration options.

Counter Space

Like any retail operation, you need a counter area where customers can pay for their purchases. For a florist shop, this space doesn't have to be large, but you do want somewhere to put the customer's purchase (which they will certainly want to see before they pay) while they are paying. And you want to have a small amount of room for some impulse items like special notecards or other decorative items to include with the bouquet or arrangement.

Merchandise Display

While other merchandise will make up only a small percentage of your overall revenue, having some room for some floral-related merchandise is just plain good business. These can be anything from unique vases to greeting cards to silk flowers and plants. Give customers reason to come into your shop and browse a little, even if they aren't in need of a special arrangement at that moment. If you pull them into your shop with some impulse item, and you get a chance to charm them, you will have gained a potential customer who will think of you the next time they do need to order flowers.

Storage

Besides places to showcase merchandise for sale, you will need ample storage space with appropriate shelving and racking in the nonshowroom area to store items like vases, stocks of floral supplies including boxes, as well as supplies of your retail items. Keep this area out of sight of customers if at all possible. Otherwise, it makes the retail space look cluttered and uninviting.

Walking Around Space

Despite wanting to pack your retail space effectively with revenue-generating items, retailers always

> ### Tip...
>
> **Smart Tip**
>
> You can learn from all retail businesses. Whenever you are shopping—at the bookstore, the grocery store, the clothing store, the sporting goods store—look around and see what the successful stores are doing. From displays to signage to traffic patterns and impulse point-of-purchase items, there are ideas you can steal and incorporate into your florist shop.

> **⚠ Beware!**
> Don't crowd your shop so full that customers feel awkward and uncomfortable trying to navigate their way around. They simply will not come back. Make your shop inviting and intriguing with just enough merchandise to keep customers interested but not so much that they fear they will break something with every move they make.

need to keep the customer's overall experience in mind. How many times have you been discouraged from browsing through a clothing rack because there simply are too many clothes jammed into the rack? You can't see any individual item, you can't pull anything off the rack, and if you manage to get something off, you certainly can't get it back on the rack. Give customers room to see things. Make a walking space from the door to your cash-out counter that is clear sailing. Tempt them off the beaten path with intriguing displays and unique items, but don't make them fear that if they buy a vase full of flowers, they might trash the place trying to squeeze out the door.

Atmosphere

You want to create a floral shop that gives off a particular feel when a customer walks in. Whatever you choose is fine—high-end, classy floral boutique, lower-priced, simple shop with lots of carnations, or somewhere in between—but know what you want to be and announce it to the world with your entire look. This includes your signage, business cards, and other marketing pieces (covered in Chapter 10) and also what your store looks like.

Part of your image will come merely from where you choose to locate your shop. From there, please your customers. If you want to charge lots of money for unusual, special-order-only flowers in unique arrangements using only the finest European glassware, you probably don't want to locate your store in the strip mall between the liquor store and the off-track betting joint. And if you dress the front of your store up in European styling, don't surprise your customers with only rickrack and country baskets for their choices when they come inside.

Know your market, and go after it with your merchandise. One of the best ways to start thinking about how you would like to dress your shop is to visit other florists. Check out

- what they use for furniture in the stores.
- how the store displays and dressing changes over time.
- where they place the checkout counters.
- what non-flower merchandise is for sale.
- what kind of music they play.
- if the shop seems to be catering to a specific area of the floral market, such as weddings.

- how you feel when you walk in. Do you feel compelled to buy something? Or does the shop décor and layout make you want to turn around and walk out? What is it about the shop that does either?

Family Affair

Do you have school-aged kids who need a place to go after school because you're not home? If you are in the same town as their school, have them come to the shop after school. Save some small jobs for your kids to do, like trimming the lower leaves off a new shipment of flowers, cleaning a shelf or putting stickers on something. Don't just let them run wild and disturb or turn away customers. Most kids love to be involved in the family business as long it is made interesting to them and they feel like they make an important contribution.

Stat Fact

Florist shop customers, according to a paper on floral merchandising by Dr. Charles R. Hall of Texas A&M University, buy cut flowers on average of six times a year with an estimated average cost per purchase of $19.75, whereas grocery store customers average a floral purchase four times a year with an average price of $6.86.

Wholesale Flowers

Starting a wholesale floral business is not for the weak of heart, because a wholesale business in an industry that is comprised of perishables like flowers requires a more sturdy constitution than most.

Storage

As in a retail shop, you need refrigerated storage. But if you put your wholesale business together efficiently, you shouldn't need lots of on-the-ground storage. As a flower wholesaler, you want to be at the flower markets buying the right quantities to be able to drive from the market to the retail customers and unload most of the contents of your refrigerated truck before you head back to the "warehouse."

The warehouse shouldn't need to be big, but it should have space for two things:

1. Some flower inventory to allow you to fill retail customers last-minute needs during the day. Retailers can only store so much. They also don't know what kind of walk-in business they might get that will wipe them out of, say, roses.

2. An office space not only to use to store business records but also to keep a computer for inventory tracking and generating marketing materials and researching information. Although the computer can take orders, you also want a phone and a person to staff the office. With the increasing proliferation of cell phones

and computerized everything, a person near a telephone may not seem as necessary, but a business with the accessible human being often still gets the customer who is on the fence about from whom to buy.

Vehicle

A wholesale operation will need a refrigerated vehicle. Let's face it, flowers are delicate. They can't be out in the summer heat, and they can't be out in the winter freezing temperatures. Your refrigerated truck will need to be on a strict maintenance schedule—downtime for your truck means downtime for your business.

> **⚠ Beware!**
> A floral wholesaler will need to keep the company's refrigerated vehicle in excellent repair—both the vehicle itself and the refrigeration unit. Don't think you are covered if you have more than one truck; if you are doing your business right, all trucks are in full swing. Find a place where you can rent a refrigerated vehicle in a pinch.

Depending on the size of the refrigerated truck your business needs to generate your projected revenue, you may also need to have a commercial driver's license to drive it.

The Markets

How does the wholesaler fit into the florist market? Imagine individual retail shops in the United States each dealing with (usually) foreign growers. Those growers would need to be willing to set up small accounts and keep track of payment. They would need to break their shipments up into tiny deliveries. The efficiencies just aren't there.

Enter the floral wholesaler. The wholesaler, instead of the grower, deals with the retail shops. The shops are located within the wholesaler's delivery region. The wholesaler sets up the shop accounts and is in regular contact with owners. The wholesaler can more readily respond to last minute needs and resolve supply problems—from delivery times to quality of merchandise. And the wholesaler can promote the growers' products to her customers.

If you have the stamina for a wholesale business, the flower wholesaler provides a very important service to the florist industry. Start-up costs, however, can be considerable, much larger than on the retail side.

Wholesale Floral Supplies

Here is the segment of the industry that may be the best of all worlds. If retailing isn't for you and you would like to be a wholesaler, here is a business that can be fun, creative, and lucrative, yet is an area of the floral industry that doesn't involve perishables and is less costly to enter.

Location

The location of a warehouse for storing your floral supplies is not nearly as crucial as the location of retail space. If you rely on your customers coming to you, it might be better to locate in an attractive area, and certainly in a safe one. And keep in mind that you, or an employee, may be spending your days there answering phones, tracking inventory, and packing orders, so the work environment needs to be appealing. Be sure the warehouse space you pick has a loading dock so you can easily receive incoming supplies and load delivery vehicles with outgoing orders.

Storage Space

First, you will need space for storing quantities of your products. There is little in the way of heating or cooling needs for most floral products, except perhaps glue, but adequate shelving that is easy to access and makes keeping track of inventory a simple task is important. Although it is not a huge expense, don't forget to include shelving in your start-up costs.

A showroom will impact your space needs. You don't have to have a showroom, but you will need a way to show customers what you have. One option is a vehicle that you fill with samples and drive to the various retail outlets. A showroom allows the retailers to come to you, but getting time to be away from a retail business can be difficult, so you may find going to your customers is the better way to go.

> **Bright Idea**
> Even warehouses need to be clean. Florists don't want to buy supplies that are dirty, dusty, and look like they have been hanging around a while. Once a year, consider having a sale and clear out anything that hasn't moved recently. Unless you can return the items and get your full money back, it is a good way to keep your shelves clear, clean, and full of fresh inventory.

If you do decide to have a showroom, you don't have to have it connected to your warehouse, although it is more handy that way. One key reason it is handier is that if your customers place orders after reviewing your goods, they can often times load up their vehicles with their orders if they are not huge.

You can also do both—have a showroom at your warehouse and open showrooms in other areas in order to expand your market. However, the more separate these aspects of your business are, the more employees you will need.

Top 10 Reasons Why Retailers Buy from Wholesale Florists

The top ten reasons retailers buy from wholesale florists are because wholesalers:

1. Stand behind their products, even if that means replacement or a full credit.

2. Offer the flexibility that allows retailers to buy in either small or large quantities.

3. Offer price discounts for quantities purchased in bulk or by standing orders.

4. Provide reasonable credit terms.

5. Introduce retailers to new products and services to help them stay competitive.

6. Allow retailers to see the product before they buy.

7. Educate retailers about important crops—from the field to the retail market—especially at holiday times.

8. Host design seminars and distribute product materials.

9. Jointly support consumer marketing programs with retailers.

10. Identify, process, and assemble products for retailers.

(From the Wholesale Florists & Florist Suppliers Assn.)

Supplies

Here is where wholesale gets fun. Florists are a perfect market for unique items. You can get creative by sniffing out unusual vases and decorative items. You also need to stock the basic florist materials—wire, foam, different types of glue, boxes, paper wrap, wedding bouquet holders, etc. And you will need to have ample supply of the standard simple vases. But you can then move on to colored vases or containers with interesting shapes. Even the standard foam and other supplies come in unique shapes, such as topiary forms and risers. And because you are in the nonperishable market, you can be a supplier of high-quality silk flowers as well.

▲

Ordering

The basics you can order and keep in stock at all times. For unique items, try getting orders ahead of time, at least enough to fill the minimum requirement for the best possible discount. When a florist wants to order something you don't normally keep in stock, take advantage of being able to fulfill a minimum with her order, and add a couple extras to the order so you can have a good variety of items to offer all customers.

A wholesale business selling floral supplies can be a great business—fun, creative, and, if you place close attention to the bottom line, plenty lucrative.

4

Market Research
and Financing

Market research for any business consists of two components: 1) where your customers come from, and 2) what other businesses like yours are in your proposed market area. Although they are in most ways two different issues, the area where you are proposing to open your florist business has to have a big enough potential customer base to support your revenue needs as well as—and here's where the connection comes—any other businesses like yours in the same market area.

Market research will be necessary for including key information in your business plan, especially if you plan to seek financing. There are many specific things to consider when you put together market research, including where you are going to draw your customers from and what other florists will be directly competitive with your business. Consider the following specific things to look for while researching each market component.

Customer Base

Where will you draw customers from for your business? The main customer base for most retail businesses can be determined by the area that the phone book reaches. Because phone books cover overlapping towns—one phone book may cover two of the same three towns as another—be sure you are listed in the Yellow Pages section of all phone books within a 30- to 40-mile radius of your business.

Will people who live 40 miles away use your flower shop when it is likely they have a flower shop within ten miles? You would think probably not, but those same people may work within ten miles of your shop. Working people often conduct much of their daily business closer to their offices than their homes. If they are at home trying to figure out where they could get an arrangement done that they could pick up the next day on their lunch break, you would want them to know about you.

For the florist business there are basically three kinds of customers:

1. *The walk-in customer*. These are rare, although you may get several a day depending on the location of your shop and how much walk-by traffic there is.

Buying flowers on impulse is certainly likely, especially if you have a display of striking cut flowers on the sidewalk. But the revenue from walk-in sales is not going to be the bulk of your revenue base. The only time this may change is during the key annual holidays when flowers are big—Valentine's Day, Easter, Mother's Day, Thanksgiving, and Christmas.

2. *The call-in order.* This is probably where the bulk of your everyday sales will come from. Is your business in a market large enough to bring you the revenue you need via called orders? Of course, Teleflora and FTD add to that revenue, but you also make only a small percentage of the overall price on those sales.

3. *Special markets.* Florists make the bulk of their revenue doing weddings and other special events. Hitch up with a few large churches with a wealthy congregation that decorates the altar each week with fresh arrangements. Tap into the local business market, and offer good prices on regular orders for arrangements for their colleagues and the customers they put up in local hotels. Get the hotels on your list as well, creating fresh arrangements for their lobbies, near elevators, etc. Special sales such as this have become a key component of the overall revenue stream of almost any retail business, large or small.

Other Businesses

If there is another retail florist already open in the area, should you automatically walk away and find another place or, if you are stuck on that market area, decide to go into another type of business? Not necessarily. If your market research determines that the market is big enough, there very well could be enough customers to support two, maybe more, retail flower shops.

Perhaps you have decided that you would like to open an upscale florist shop offering high-priced arrangements. Your market research turns up another upscale florist on the other side of town, a town of around 30,000 people. There may not be enough everyday business for two upscale florists in a small city. But there are ways you can distinguish your floral business from another. And you can choose to target a niche or two—weddings, funerals, religious services, special events—within the industry that would help your shop not have to rely totally on everyday orders.

Bright Idea
Marketing classes at business schools and local colleges and universities are often looking for real-life projects to take on. If the timing is right, contact the head of the appropriate department and see if there is a class that would like to help you by doing market research for your start-up flower shop.

There are many reasons that customers choose one shop over another. One of those key reasons is the people who run the shop—the owner, the manager, the daily personnel. You will automatically have a clientele from your friends, family, and their networks of local friends and families. Practice on them to find ways to draw other clientele, build your customer base, and set yourself apart from your competition.

Of course, you don't want to set yourself up to fail. In your research of other businesses within your target area, don't just count how many there are. Do a thorough examination of these businesses. Walk into them, shop in them, order flowers from them. Find out how they do things so you can do things differently—or the same but better. Explore what they do right and what they do wrong. Mimic the good things, avoid the bad. Then when you go to create your marketing materials, you can point out the things that distinguish you from the competition.

Don't print on your brochure "Flo's Florists has more design experience than Flower City does." But do say something like "Flo's Florists' designer spent three years studying Ikebana in Japan. Let us create a unique arrangement for your special occasion." Chances are Flower City doesn't have an Ikebana-trained florists. Find uniqueness and flaunt it.

Doing Market Research

There are several questions you want to find answers for when conducting market research:

- *Who is going to buy from your flower shop?* A lot of this depends on how you design your business. Young, hip lawyers are probably not going to be attracted to a business whose storefront has African violets amidst crocheted quilts in pastel colors and that looks like it is after the silver-haired, older woman crowd. But window displays that regularly include bright colors, striking arrangements, mannekins painted purple, and strobe lights will bring in a totally different clientele. Know who you want to do business with and target them accordingly.

- *Where will you find your customers?* Do you need a large mailing to local office buildings? Perhaps you will need to place a regular ad in the Saturday paper.

Learn where your target market members go to find out about things they need, and be sure your store name appears before their eyes when they are looking to send flowers.

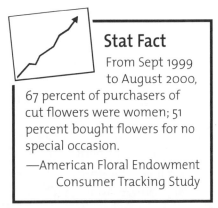
- *What price range will your target market bear?* The good thing about the flower business is that all price ranges are possible. Although flowers aren't a big ticket item to begin with, they also are not a necessity. So even though an occasional arrangement is probably not going to bankrupt most people, they are bought using disposable income. Because this is an industry that can serve all economic groups, you should be sure to have all price ranges of arrangements available.

- *What other businesses might cut into your market share?* For example, are there several grocery stores, small and large, in the area? Have they expanded their flower sections to larger areas with more unique offerings? Herb shops often have significant dried flower sections; other gift stores can specialize in dried or silk flowers or have sidelines you were thinking of carrying.

Trade Associations

The florist industry's many trade associations can help tremendously in researching the market in the area you are considering. They may not have general information on the street or even town location, but they will have statistics on small-town retail shops, current buying trends, and other key marketing information that will help you make decisions and understand your potential market area. Join trade associations even before you set up shop, and use their information databases, magazines, and newsletters to your advantage.

Beware!
Even if you may think you don't have time to attend chamber of commerce and other business group events, you can't afford not to. Remember, you may have started your business to be a florist and arrange flowers, but you also are a business owner. Keep that in mind no matter what industry you are in.

Online

Of course, today the internet is a key market research tool. Provided you have a computer, you can sit in the comfort of your own home and research the floral industry around the country. Take notes and print out key pieces of information. As you dig down into a web site, you can lose track of the original source, so be sure to start a favorites folder for any floral web sites you don't want to lose track of.

Be a snoop and follow all leads into things you think might be of interest. This kind of searching can help you find niches you hadn't thought of and give you ideas for your business setup. It can also help you gain valuable information that you can use to fill out your business plan.

Search general words like "florist," "florist supplies," "florist associations," "flowers," and "flower arranging," and see where they lead. (See the Appendix for specific web sites and other contact information.) There should be plenty of general information; drill down to more specific information from there.

Financing

Once you have targeted your market and have it down on paper along with the other key business details, you are ready to add the financing information to your business plan. There are several possible ways to obtain financing: banks, private investors, friends, family, minority- and women-owned business assistance programs, the Small Business Administration, personal savings, and selling personal assets. You should be prepared to examine all financing options that are potentially available to you.

Beware!

Undercapitalization is a key reason that small businesses fail. Be realistic about your start-up expenses and your potential revenue for the first two to three years. Don't get a loan that gives you a debt that is impossible to service, but don't think you are going to succeed on less than you think you need to get a good foothold in your business. You might, but it will be a struggle and the odds are against an undercapitalized business.

Banks

Banks are not fond of loaning money for retail start-ups. The statistics on failed retail businesses are too high for their comfort levels. Don't rule them out, however. If you make your business plan compelling enough, and you do your homework to make it clear you are serious about succeeding, you may get a more positive reaction.

Start with your personal banker at the bank (or banks) where you have done business for a while. This person will probably be more receptive to your request for a meeting. It's hard not to be emotional about being turned down, but keep in mind that if a bank rejects

Bright Idea

When you sign up for the SBA's SCORE program, your retired business mentor probably won't be a former flower shop owner. However, he or she probably will have been in the retail sector. Keep an open mind to what you can learn from other parts of the retail industry and how you can apply it to the florist business.

your loan request, rarely is the reason personal. Often they think businesses are good ideas but the industry or retail in general is just too risky for the bank's portfolio of business loans.

If you do get a meeting, be prepared to include other sources of financing in your business plan. Even if the bank offers to finance your business, it is unlikely to give you the entire start-up capital you will need. In fact, banks often look for business owners to be willing to invest considerable personal assets along with the bank's financing to start up a business. However, banks will also be wary of your stretching yourself completely to your limit—this leaves little fallback room in case of future need. Include potential loans (ask first!) from friends and family investors. A couple thousand here, a couple thousand there, and you can be on your way.

Partners

Partnering can be a plausible way to finance a start-up business. First off, partners can be silent or active. A silent partner loans the money, has little if anything to do with the day-to-day business, and just makes money from your repayment of the loan or eventual sale of the business. Active partners can be 50/50 partners in the business, doing 50 percent of the work, taking in 50 percent of the profits, and taking on 50 percent of the risk. This can be a very good solution for a number of reasons:

- If you choose the right partner, he can bring assets to the business in the form of skills and experience that can complement your own and make your business more appealing and more stable in the eyes of investors.

- Having a partner can mean that you and your partner can each work hard in the business but also take a day off or even the occasional longer vacation knowing someone who is as commited as you is minding the store.

- Finding a partner who complements your own skills can make your business that much more successful. If you both want to be the main florist, you will probably have problems—and too much overlap of skills for a small store. But if you are a skilled florist and your partner is an artist with a flair for making awesome window displays, you can each share the more mundane tasks and really create a store with impact.

- A partner brings his or her own circle of family and friends into the immediate customer base.

These are all good reasons to have a partner. The main problem with a partner is that you need to be sure she is someone with whom you are very compatible. Many a good friendship has been ruined through business partnerships. And you need to think about whether you can manage to live on the decreased revenue if your partner is taking half the profits. (The flip side of that is with a partner you might be able to halve the time between start-up and actually being profitable.)

If you approach partnerships very, very carefully, draw up legal agreements, and are completely up front with each other about everything, it can be a win-win situation. Having someone who is also intimately involved with your business can double the enjoyment and cut the bad times by half.

Private Investors

Private investors and venture capital firms are probably not realistic sources of capital for a retail flower shop. Venture capitalists prefer to get into businesses on a larger scale, particularly in high-tech and manufacturing. It may make more sense if you are planning to open a wholesale flower business, but again, the perishable aspects of the business may scare these kinds of investors away.

> ### Smart Tip
>
> Tip...
>
> When it comes to looking for financing to start your business, banks and other potential lenders will look more confidently on the business plan that shows a florist with some experience. Starting and running your own business is hard enough without having to learn the industry from scratch at the same time. And if you have been working in the industry, you have a better sense if being a florist is the right profession for you. Lenders want to increase the odds that you are going to stay in the business long enough for your start-up shop to become established and profitable.

Friends and Family

Because of the reluctance of conventional loan sources to get into retail, friends and family are a common source of start-up capital for a retail business. Although these sources are important, they are not without potential disastrous results. If either a friend or a family member lends you money for your business, be perfectly clear how and when you plan to repay the loan. Don't rely on your memory. Write the details down, and each keep a copy so that both parties have written record of what you agreed on. Be prepared for the relationship to go sour, especially if the business fails, but if you are honest throughout, you should be able to salvage your relationship even then.

The one drawback that can be troubling about borrowing from friends and family is that you can feel this tinge of obligation/guilt every time they walk into your shop. Learn to avoid that—unless you held them up at gunpoint (in which case you have other issues. . .). They lent you the money of their own free will. Many people do this in order to be vicariously involved in something they wish they had the guts to do or were in the right situation to do. Be happy to see them come into your store. They are thrilled to be even a small part of it!

The Business
Side of Flowers

You may not consider yourself "good with numbers," but having your own business requires you to become at least proficient. You will probably never enjoy finances as much as flowers, but all business owners should be intimately involved with the financial side of their businesses. You can choose to hire someone else to take care of the nitty gritty, but you still want to understand the basics of your business's financial setup and what it all means to its success. Without a financial core, business is not business; it's volunteerism.

You simply won't be in business long if you don't appreciate the implications of its financial foundation. You need to buy a good delivery vehicle, have credit with your suppliers, and know the logic of how large an inventory to have on hand.

There are a few things to decide about your financial future before you begin to arrange the first flowers. You should have your books ready to record expenditures and revenue the first time you spend or take in money for the business.

Get Classy

One way to learn the basics of accounting and finances for small business is to take an accounting class. Check with your local Small Business Development Center (SBDC), which may offer small-business accounting classes or keep a list of classes offered through local community colleges or continuing education programs at local universities.

Don't set yourself up to fail! Sign up for basic classes, something designed to teach the fundamentals of the financial framework of a small business. You don't need to know how to read the financial report of a multi-million dollar international corporation if you plan to start up a one-person retail florist shop in a small town.

Another way to start learning about small-business finance is to take a class in writing business plans—financial projections will be part of that plan.

Cycles of the Financial Moon

First, you need to decide what your fiscal year will be. It depends on how you set up your business. Sole proprietors should choose the calendar year as their fiscal year. Business income for the sole proprietorship will be reported as Schedule C on your personal income tax return, which is filed according to the calendar year. (More about the dreaded "T" word later.)

Corporations operate under a different tax structure, and can choose a fiscal year according to the logic of their business/industry. For example, the florist industry's busiest quarter is the last one of the year. The second quarter might be next, with Mother's Day and Easter, depending on whether Easter falls in the first or second quarter in any given year.

Retail usually has its fiscal year the same as the calendar year, which means that as much as half of its annual sales comes at the end of the fiscal year, which can cause some nail-biting moments.

Keeping the Books

Unless you are planning to create a mega-florist from the start, you should be able to do your own day-to-day bookkeeping without things getting out of hand. Anyone who has worked at all before knows the old mantra: Keep every receipt for every dime you spend that has anything to do with the business. You don't have to keep your ledger in your wallet but do gather those receipts in a common place and record them in the ledger at least once a week so the chore doesn't become a huge one.

Your Checkbook

For the small retail business, your business checkbook will probably be your most important financial tool, at least in the beginning. No matter what size business you start, plan to have a separate business account. There is nothing that looks less professional—except perhaps having the kids answer the phone—than using the same checking account for your personal finances and your business. And you will make it harder on yourself to keep things separate, like deposits that are personal money and those for business.

Get a separate business checking account from the start, and pay for everything with it, even if you use the account's cash card instead of writing a check. It doesn't have to be an actual "business account." Another personal checking account will do; just make it separate from your personal business. Have your business name printed at the top to add professionalism.

Tracking Money the Old-Fashioned Way

If you like a pen-and-paper approach, you can keep your books using the old-fashioned ledger notebooks that you can still purchase in any office supply or stationery store. Keep a column for expenses and one for income. At the end of each month or quarter or whenever you have agreed upon, hand these ledgers over to your accountant who will review them, balance them, let you know how much you still have in your checking account, and depending on the agreements you've made, perhaps even make suggestions on how to better keep your records or save money. A well-kept ledger can tell you a lot at a glance about the day-to-day status of your business.

Bright Idea
Although you will use your computer extensively in your florist business, remember that the florist business is still very much a customer-service business.

Software

In this computer age, you are more likely turn to computer software for book-keeping. Two commonly used programs are QuickBooks and Microsoft Office. There are others with less well-known names, like Big E-Z Monthly Bookkeeping for Small Businesses. Ask other business owners what they use and find the one that best suits you.

The main thing you need to keep in mind is that while these programs do many calculations and other useful things at the touch of a few keys on the keyboard, they still require you to set them up in the first place and input the basic information, both initially and on an ongoing basis.

So if you are thinking that computerizing your books and doing it yourself is the easy way out, think again. There are some clear time advantages to business software, but no matter which method you choose, you will need to regularly step away from the arranging counter and spend time on the bookkeeping end of things. Set aside a chunk of time to start, and then keep it up on an ongoing basis, maybe an hour weekly and a morning monthly—or whatever fits your schedule.

Be sure to keep these software products up to date by logging on to their web sites periodically and signing up for their updates. Although the bookkeeping products probably won't have much in the way of updates, the tax products will have constant updates to keep up with the changing tax codes.

If you know yourself well enough to know that you are not going to set aside this time to feed your bookkeeping software, then simply hire an accountant. The upcoming meeting with your accountant will force you to pull together your information, and you will have a person who will be nudging you to keep appropriate records and provide him with the necessary information to keep your finances accurate and up to date. Most accountants who focus on small business are not expensive and will probably save you as much money as they cost.

Accounting Methods

There are two basic accounting methods: accrual and cash accounting.

1. *Accrual.* This method of accounting is used in businesses where inventory is a factor. This is significant for both the wholesale and retail floral business; although the delivery part of the retail business is service-oriented, you are still selling a product that took inventory to create.

2. *Cash.* Cash accounting simply means that you record an invoice as revenue when you send it out and you record an expense when you receive the bill that

your business is supposed to pay. It is a very simple means of accounting.

Making a Statement

Businesses use several statements to get an overview of their businesses and their financial status.

- *Profit and loss statements (P&L).* This statement allows you to get a monthly picture of where your business stands that month, for the year to date, and compared to this time last year (either for the month or the year to date).

- *Cash flow statement.* This handy little statement lets you know how much money is coming into your business compared to how much is going out.

- *Balance sheet.* The balance sheet balances all your business's assets against all its liabilities. How much you own is compared to how much you owe. This crucial statement lets you know how your business is faring financially at any given moment in time, giving you the ability to make some changes to shift the balance more in your favor. Some changes you can make to tip this balance include

  - increasing your prices,
  - getting a more economical delivery vehicle,
  - reducing the range of your deliveries to spend less time on the road and less on gas,
  - increasing the range of your deliveries if you don't feel you are reaching a large enough market,
  - always requiring payment at time of services, and
  - finding new suppliers of the things you need to keep on hand.

You will, by the way, have created all of these statements for your business plan, although because at that stage they are not based on actual numbers but on projected figures, they are known as "pro formas."

Stat Fact
According to the web site flobiz now.com, there are:

- 26,200 retail flower shops
- 23,000 supermarkets selling flowers
- 16,432 nurseries and garden centers
- 1,000 wholesalers
- 11,480 domestic floriculture growers

Accountant

The bookkeeping and tax software may be enough while you are still quite small. But as your business grows, you definitely should consider hiring an accountant to help you keep your records organized, adequate, and useful. While an accountant is an additional expense, it is a worthy investment. You don't have to use your accountant on a daily basis. Quarterly is probably enough to begin with. You can always increase your accountant's input to monthly when you have reached a certain level of revenue. A good accountant will let you know when the time is right.

The important thing is that the accountant will keep you on track with your financial framework. Tax time will be easier. Growth will be easier. Getting additional capital will be easier. You can be ready to jump on unexpected opportunities—a competing business for sale, a great deal on closeout supplies you can use—instead of first having to recreate your financial history because you didn't keep good records and weren't able to immediately present your business from a financial perspective.

Set up an introductory meeting with at least a couple of accountants. Pick someone with whom you feel comfortable. You can weed out some possibilities over the phone. One key question to ask your potential accountants is what kind of small business experience they have in general and whether they have any particular experience in the floral industry. Then, meet your finalists in person. There may be a small fee for this meeting, but it is well worth it to go confidently into what you hope will be a long-term relationship.

Smart Tip

If you allow a business to establish an account for business orders, offer a discount to the company's entire staff to use for personal orders. This can encourage them to come to you with their floral business instead of someone else.

Tax Accountant

Smart Tip

If you have an employee, you need an EIN— Employee Identification Number—issued by the IRS. You can apply online at www.irs.gov. Or you can send in form SS-4. It is simple, fairly quick, and absolutely necessary for anything but the smallest sole proprietorship.

You can't get around it—being a business owner complicates tax time. This is another instance where hiring an accountant comes in handy. You need, however, to be sure your accountant is a *tax* accountant, not solely a bookkeeper. There are so many rules and layers to tax laws that having a tax-savvy accountant will pay for itself in sheer savings on aspirin alone.

In its attempt to become more customer-friendly, the IRS has a fantastic web site that falls in the category of "more than you ever want or need to know." But if it involves federal taxes, it is there. You can download publications and forms to read on screen or print out, which can save you on the eve of your tax filing due date if you are scrambling to meet the deadline.

One IRS publication that all small-business entrepreneurs should download or get a copy of is the *Tax Guide for Small Businesses* (Publication 334). Don't worry about remembering it all—although there will be a nonnegotiable test every year!

Auto Expenses

Beware!

Don't fall into the trap of never paying yourself out of your business earnings. While it is important for a start-up business to dump a lot of its revenue back into the business, burnout is one of the top reasons that small businesses fail. So, if you work 80 hours a week, you should at least take enough money out of the business checkbook to treat yourself to a spa visit or whatever you find will recharge your batteries for the next 80-hour work week!

Because deliveries can make up a substantial portion of a retail florist shop's revenue, you will need to keep detailed records of your delivery vehicle use. Ideally, the delivery vehicle will be a dedicated vehicle, not your personal car, so keeping records will be fairly easy.

You can record actual expenses for your vehicle—oil changes, tires, gas, etc. However, if at least to start out you use the same vehicle for both personal and business use, it may be more expedient to simply use the IRS mileage rate (it changes almost every year, so be sure to check) because otherwise you will need to pro rate all expenses, which makes it more complicated than it needs to be.

The key point is that with this kind of business where deliveries are critical, automobile use is a significant expense and should be taken very seriously, recording every possible cent you spend. This is not only important for tax purposes but, as is discussed

COGS in the Floral Wheel

As a business owner, you will hear a lot about Cost of Goods Sold, fondly known as COGS. COGS differentiates from overhead expenses, which are fixed. COGS will increase with increased revenue because every time you provide your service or sell a product, it cost a certain amount in expenses.

elsewhere in this book, this is one of those places where hidden costs can eat away at your profits and you can't pinpoint exactly where the money is disappearing.

Client Invoices and Receipts

Even if you require payment up front (which you should), you always want to provide your customers with an invoice or receipt. This allows both of you to keep a record of purchases—especially if you cultivate a large business customer base.

A software program to create invoices and receipts will also serve a dual purpose for marketing. Many are capable of keeping track of customer purchase history so when a customer calls wanting a delivery, you can look to see if you already have directions to the same home or business and impress your customer with saving him or her time. And customers simply like to know that businesses remember them. Good record-keeping not only helps you organize your business from a financial standpoint, but it also gives you opportunities to excel at building customer service and client relationships.

Best Practices for Small Businesses

When running a small business, there are several best practices that will help your business lean in the direction of success. Here are six:

1. *Respect the financial side of things.* Don't be embarrassed about making money and don't be shy about collecting debts. No customer should expect your business to be unprofitable. Set your fees at a rate the market will bear; if you have set your business up logically, that should bring you the cash flow you need to create and maintain a good business. Give away this little service and that half hour of consulting time, and you are eating away at the time you have to service good-paying customers.

2. *Create a business plan, no matter how small your start-up.* A business plan gives you a guide to base all decisions on and against which to measure your success.

3. *Borrow as little as possible but as much as you need.* Undercapitalization is the big reason for small business failure. Mary B. of Wyoming Florists says, "Don't forget about the start-up time when you aren't selling anything." This is true whether it is a new business or expansion of an existing business. You need

to be able to set your business up and keep your business running in order to get customers to bring in revenue and make your business a financial success.

4. *Maintain personal health insurance.* If your spouse has a job that provides benefits for you both, excellent. Many small business owners go without health insurance; this is simply a disaster waiting to happen. Don't be without at least catastrophic insurance that would cover large hospital and emergency room bills. Another part of your health insurance strategy is to have disability insurance that provides some level of coverage if you are injured and can't work. Disability insurance can be quite expensive, but if you shop around, you can find plans that provide you with reasonable coverage at reasonable rates.

5. *Be realistic about the amount of business you take on.* Burnout is one of the top factors in why small businesses close—the owner/manager simply wears out. No small business owner can afford to be accused of being lazy, but committing 18 hours a day, six or seven days a week is exhausting, plain and simple. If you plan to start a business, make it phenomenally successful, and sell it within two years, maybe that would work. But if you are planning to be in it for the long haul, pace yourself. Start slowly and increase your business as you gain experience and capital.

6. *Hire employees sparingly.* In the retail florist business, Mary B. admits it is difficult not to have employees right from the start. But paychecks, social security contributions, workers' compensation, and unemployment taxes add up fast. When you think it is time for an employee, first consider if there are other options. For instance, Mary B. uses a delivery service to cover deliveries outside her immediate zip code. This way she can expand her business to include the greater Cincinnati area, even across the river into northern Kentucky without hiring an employee. When you decide an employee is necessary, do a thorough financial breakdown, preferably with your accountant, and make sure the employee will pay for herself in a short time.

Payment Options

With a retail florist business that takes a lot of orders over the phone, you will need to have the ability to accept many credit cards. Visa and MasterCard are a must, Discover is probably important, and despite the fact that the fees are higher, American Express is critical if you plan to cater to the business customer. Visa and MasterCard are set up with your bank. American Express deals directly. Both entail a per-charge fee, usually a percentage of the order amount. Again, American Express charges a higher percentage than the other major credit cards, but it is well worth the extra because this is the card most businesses provide their employees.

Checks are another story. Although check-verifying services can provide immediate verification that a check is probably good, these days, a client should be able to easily use a debit card, which processes the charge immediately like a credit card.

> **Beware!**
> While growth is the desired goal of almost any business, beware of growing too fast—too many customers, too many expenses, too many employees. Mary B. of Wyoming Florists recommends, "Don't think too big to start." You can always expand. And when you do, plan your expansion carefully. All businesses measure growth differently, but do measure your growth regularly—and always use your business plan as a guide for growth.

Policies

Every business that deals with customers (which is every business, small or large) needs to establish policies, which need to be adequately communicated to your customers, and they need to be followed rigorously. There will be exceptions, of course, but if every instance becomes an exception, then there are no longer exceptions because there really are no rules.

Policies are often focused on payment and money-related activities, but there are other areas where you may find you need to have policies. One big one in the retail floral business is deliveries. Will you have a range that you will not go outside of? Is there a time of the day before which same-day delivery orders need to come in?

Not only do you need to stick to your policies, but also be sure anyone who works for you knows the policies and adheres to them as well.

Collections

Retail florists should do most of their business on a cash-only basis. However, if you develop some large, regular clients, especially business clients, you may want to offer an account. Although you wouldn't think that a large business would have trouble paying bills to a small retail shop, don't be surprised. There are several things to establish up front to have a successful relationship with a business account:

- *Establish up front the turnaround time for payment.* Will you bill once a month? Once a week? And how long do you give for payment? You might want to have the payment due in the same timeframe as the billing cycle—e.g., if you bill the client once a month, give him 30 days to pay his bill. But keep in mind that in this scenario, you may be waiting as much as 60 days to get payment on an order that came in at the beginning of the month.

- *Besides establishing a billing and payment cycle up front, establish an account limit.* Even large companies have gone out of business, and a small business like yours does not want to be left holding a big bag.
- *Be sure to request a list of approved users of the account.* Just VPs? Better yet, ask the account to have just one person—for instance, the secretary/receptionist—call in orders and let that person work from a list of who is approved to use the account. That way you can deal with just one person.

Paying Yourself

The majority of small business owners go for years without paying themselves out of the business. They dump all their profits back into the business, which is basically a wise thing to do. If you can afford to, by all means build the company up as much as you can.

Under most circumstances, you should probably set yourself up for not needing to take anything out of the business for the first year. But there does come a point when you want to give yourself at least some pay. If you are independently wealthy, then pay yourself enough for some "mad money" or donate something to charity or give some to your kids or grandkids or nieces and nephews. Perhaps your spouse has a fantastic job that provides for all the household needs—great, pay yourself enough to do some long-wanted home renovations or buy an indulgence like a pool table or new kitchen cabinets.

The upshot is, don't let the business drain you to the point of feeling resentful about it. There is some reward to knowing that your business is providing some financial return, even if it is just dinner out a couple times a week!

If you *need* to get a paycheck out of the business, you must decide how big your paycheck needs to be, then figure out how much revenue you need to take in to pay yourself that much, and then figure out where that amount will come from.

Obtaining Financing

If you need to approach a lender for a loan, having financial projections and statements in order and presenting them professionally as part of your loan request can get you far. Applying for a loan can be stressful—it is often difficult to get beyond the emotional part of wanting to start your business, making it hard to understand a

Start-Up Expense List

Pre-Start-Up

Market research (phone calls, subscriptions to trade journals, trips to florists, professional association memberships)	$
Legal and accounting services	$
Start-up advertising	$
Web site design	$
Lease deposit (security, first/last month)	$
Leasehold improvements	$
Utility deposits	$
Equipment	
Walk-in cooler	$
Reach-in cooler	$
Delivery vehicle	$
Floral Supplies (vases, foam, glue, etc.)	$
Store supplies (gift cards, receipts, pens/pencils, cleaners, etc.)	$
Store furnishings (display pedestals, chairs, rugs, etc.)	$
Perishables	$
Subtotal	**$**
Miscellaneous (roughly 10% of subtotal)	$
Total	**$**

lender's reluctance to give you a business loan. Being prepared with a full complement of financial statements in your business plan will save you some headaches.

Capital Concerns

There are two kinds of money you will need for your business at the start-up stage:

1. *Start-up money*. This is the amount of money you will need to open your doors for business. What kind of florist business you decide to start will greatly impact how much this needs to be. You will need at least three months' rent up front (first, last, and a security deposit in the form of one month's rent is common), although having six months rent upfront would be wiser. You will need cash to buy inventory until you can establish accounts—many wholesalers require new businesses to pay upfront for their first order and establish an account with a low limit after that. You will need to set up phone and other utilities, get credit card processing paraphernalia, as well as a cash register, etc. You will, of course, need to buy some supplies—vases, ribbon, packaging material, and flowers. And you will need the proper fixtures to outfit your space—arranging counter, checkout counter, display racks, reach-in cooler for cut flowers and small arrangements for immediate sale, and walk-in cooler for inventory and larger orders. And you will need to purchase a delivery vehicle, which may or may not be a separate auto loan. Basically, your start-up capital should be enough to open your doors to business. See the Start-Up Expense List on page 44.

2. *Operating capital*. This is the money required to keep your business running, at least until it is generating enough income to bring in revenue. The goal is, of course, to have the business generate its own operating capital—and eventually a profit, too. Until this happens, the delivery vehicle will need gas, the phone bill will need to be paid, the shop lights will need to come on, and employees will need to get a paycheck regularly.

6

Insurance and Legal Matters

You are dealing with pretty flowers and people's emotions, no need to worry about insurance, right? Wrong. You always need to be sure to protect yourself. There isn't a business in existence that doesn't need legal protection. And there are a few other insurance policies to consider as well.

You can do all the research yourself and obtain all the different insurances you need, but it is much more efficient to use an insurance broker. Although one broker may not handle all the types of insurances you need, many deal in several different kinds of insurance. A good broker will send a notice of upcoming policy renewal needs and a breakdown of your options. Look for a broker who works on commission paid through the insurance companies he sells for. Most deal with several different insurance companies, so although they are selling the companies they work with, you do get several options.

Liability Insurance

This should be dealt with first because it is so important. With a retail store, liability insurance is needed to cover events like someone falling in your shop, having a vase fall on someone's head, or odd things happening that you were certain could never happen. If a recipient of a flower arrangement has a severe allergic reaction to a particular flower or a bee on the arrangement stings a person allergic to bees who then dies, you may not think that logically it is your fault (it isn't)—but in the land of liability lawsuits, lawyers come after every possible connection to the event. You can't stop them from suing, but you can protect yourself from a lawsuit wiping you out.

If you are operating your florist business from home and your zoning allows your business to have customers come to your property, be sure either your homeowner's insurance has a rider covering business practice or you take out a separate business liability policy.

Disability Insurance

Any business owner or self-employed person should attempt to obtain a disability insurance policy that covers you if you can no longer do the job you are trained to do. Short-term disability—which tends to cover you immediately—is often prohibitively

Tip...

Smart Tip

Find an insurance broker who will look for the best insurance policies for you. Some brokers deal only in one or two types of insurance, but they have access to information at their fingertips that would take you hours and hours of research to dig out. The insurance broker will also come to know your priorities—for instance, whether you want the best health insurance for a reasonable cost or whether you simply want catastrophic insurance as inexpensively as you can get it. At renewal time, your broker should send you a menu of options and recommendations based on his knowledge of the current status of the insurance market and what you need or want out of a policy.

expensive. But you should be able to find a long-term policy that falls within the realm of affordability. Long-term disability insurance often doesn't kick in for six months after you become disabled, so you need to consider what you can do to cover yourself during that six months. And you need to know that most disability insurance policies do not pay you 100 percent of the amount you were making, so know that up front and be prepared to make necessary cuts in your budget.

Health Insurance

Many self-employed people scrimp when it comes to health insurance. Yes, it is a large chunk of money to pay each month. But the results of just one major illness can put you under financially—your income is reduced for the time you are ill and the medical bills can be astronomical, making the cost of health insurance seem like a mere pittance.

Consider dental insurance as well. Although all the bills do add up, dental insurance is not very expensive. And keep in mind that you can't just acquire it when you find out you have a large dental procedure that needs to be done—most insurers require you to have had the policy for two years before major work.

Auto Insurance

If you have a retail florist business in which deliveries are key, you need a delivery vehicle and therefore auto insurance. If you are planning to use your personal vehicle, at least in the beginning, be sure your insurance company knows you are using it for business purposes and pay any rider fees accordingly. You don't want to get in an accident during a delivery, try to pretend you were on personal business, and find out that the person you hit saw you take your magnetic "Sue's Flowers" off the side of your car. To be a successful small business person, you cannot be deceitful in any way, and besides, there is just no point in taking chances on something that could wipe out your business.

Legal Issues

Don't be deceived into thinking you won't have a need for legal support. Even the smallest business encounters legal issues. This doesn't have to mean lawsuits or anything negative—there are simply some fundamental legal matters involved with any business.

Corporate Structure

The first major legal decision you made about your business came when you decided which business structure you would set up: sole proprietorship, partnership, or incorporation. That choice has a huge impact on how any legal issues are handled and resolved. The choice of sole proprietorship makes things the most simple—and it also means that all of your personal belongings are at risk. Incorporating is the most complex and perhaps protects the individual owner the most, but it is also more expensive and more complicated when legal issues arise.

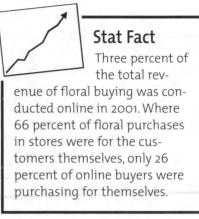

Stat Fact

Three percent of the total revenue of floral buying was conducted online in 2001. Where 66 percent of floral purchases in stores were for the customers themselves, only 26 percent of online buyers were purchasing for themselves.

Service Contracts

Although most floral businesses won't involve service contracts, there are some that do, such as providing ongoing landscaping services for either businesses or homes or for providing in-office regular plant care services. And if your business focuses on weddings or even if you do just a wedding here or there, this service does need a contract.

If you feel uncomfortable having customers sign legal contracts for services, you need to get over it. A written contract for your services makes it clear what services you will provide, when you will provide them, what is expected of your client, who pays for what supplies if appropriate, when payment is expected, and what happens if payment is not made in a timely manner.

The contract should outline your fee structure and include a limited liability statement. And you can include a warranty of your services if you desire.

Don't simply buy a pad of legal contracts at the office supply store. Your business is unique, each client has unique needs, and your contract should be able to reflect those. Hire an attorney to write up a basic contract that you can amend for each client as appropriate. While attorney's fees can add up fast, they are well worth it for a customized service contract that you will use over and over. And as your business matures and expands, you can have your attorney tweak your contract to include any changes in your business.

Some potential legal issues should be addressed in your contract, such as:

- What should happen in the event that you or an employee gets hurt on the client's premises?
- If the business owner purchases her own plants for you to either install outside or take care of in the office, who is liable if they all die?

Don't wait for things to happen to address them. In the emotional and sometimes heated aftermath of a problem, you will wish these things were covered ahead of time—in writing.

Employees

If you want to keep your business as simple as possible, don't hire employees! They present an unavoidable level of complication. But if you want to grow your business, both in revenue and services provided, or if you want to concentrate on the part of the business that you love and are skilled at, employees will probably be a necessity. They do, however, complicate a business—from legal requirements to taxes to personality conflicts.

There are other ways to consider getting help when your business is expanding beyond your ability to keep up. Subcontractors (who work for themselves, not you; also called independent contractors) can be a great interim or even permanent step to taking on more business. In the retail or service florist business, the most likely independent contractor you might hire would be a skilled florist. In landscaping, you may hire a landscape designer on a project, and you then implement the designer's plan. The other way to deal with this, instead of hiring someone, is to acquire the skills yourself by taking classes and perhaps apprenticing to someone, although there is simply only so much one person can take on.

Noncompete and Confidentiality Agreements

If you hire an independent contractor, that person probably also contracts himself out to other florist shops. You don't want your subcontractor telling his other employers details he may learn about your business. A confidentiality agreement would cover this as well as other things, like not providing copies of contracts and other forms you have paid your attorney to create for your business.

Noncompete agreements simply state that an employee cannot start his own florist business in your market and, having had access to your client base, usurp your clients. If you do not have employees, this is a nonissue. Subcontractors do not work for you and because their business revolves around working for people in your industry, you can't very well have them sign a noncompete agreement. That said, you certainly can include a line in your subcontractor agreement that points out that your client list is the property of your business.

Remember, employees in small businesses are often testing the waters for whether or not they would like to start their own such business. You yourself may have done that. Give your employees the feeling that they can be open to that—chances are they do not plan to start a business in your market anyway. And an employee who is looking to learn the business is typically very eager to learn and will work exceptionally hard.

Nothing can prevent a previous employee or subcontractor from soliciting your clients to their new business. However, a signed agreement is a legal document in which they explicitly agreed not to do this, so if he does, you then have to decide whether or not it is worth pursuing legal action.

Workers' Compensation

If you have an employee, you must carry workers' compensation, which covers employees if they get injured while performing their job responsibilities. The purpose is to avoid lawsuits resulting from on-the-job injuries. Workers' compensation is administered under both federal and state statutes.

Finding an Attorney

Don't wait until you need an attorney to find one. If you own a business, you will need an attorney at some point for something. Here are some ways to find the attorney who is best for you:

○ Ask friends and family for referrals.

○ Call and chat with the attorney or the office receptionist. Get a sense of how they conduct business and what kind of reception you might get if you call.

○ Make sure you pick someone who has small business experience and is more likely to be sensitive to the legal needs of a small business owner.

○ Look for an attorney who has background in your type of business, whether it is wholesale, retail, or service.

○ Find out upfront what the attorney's rates are, what the standard fees are, how payment is expected, whether or not you can pay with credit cards, etc. Don't let the money part of it, which can be substantial, surprise you.

○ Last but far from least, be sure the personality of the attorney is one with which you feel comfortable and confident. You don't want to avoid consulting with your attorney just because you don't like to talk with her.

IRS Obligations

As an employer, your are obligated to withhold a certain amount for income taxes, usually a percentage based on the information the employee provides on a W-4 form filled out at hiring. You also must withhold Social Security/Medicare taxes (that famous FICA line on the W-2). Not only do you withhold the employee's share, but you, the employer, also match that amount.

But wait, there's more. With employees, Uncle Sam also dips into your profits by requiring that you pay unemployment taxes. Check the IRS site (or with your tax accountant) for the current amount you need to withhold.

You may need to make these payments monthly, depending on how much the total is. The IRS likes to make sure you keep up and don't get socked with a huge amount due all at once that you can't manage to come up with.

If you are going to have employees, be sure to keep up these employment-related tax payments. You can really see how it pays to calculate just how much additional business an employee is going to bring it and if it is worth the additional expense. (Don't forget to calculate the expense of additional fees with your accountant and, potentially, your attorney.)

Ultimately, if your business growth is pointing to the need for an employee, by all means start the hiring process. But don't take on the costs unless they are necessary. Review your business plan regularly and be sure that employees are part of the plan and are necessary for the level of expansion and growth you hope to obtain by a given time.

Outfitting a Flower Shop

Furnishing a retail shop is where you can have some real fun. Creativity is the name of the game here. You can spend as little or as much as your budget allows. There is very little a flower shop needs in the way of necessities. I'll cover those first. Then I'll go on to discuss areas that are open to broad interpretation.

The Flower Shop Necessities

Some things just can't be avoided. Flowers need refrigeration, your work area will need running water and a sizeable work table, and customers will need to know exactly where to checkout. All of these things have their own specific considerations.

Walk-In Cooler

Unless you are opening a teeny weeny retail space with a teeny weeny budget and a teeny weeny projected revenue, a walk-in cooler is a necessity. That said, there are all ranges of sizes and prices you will encounter.

The retail space you choose will have a great impact on the size of walk-in that you need. If you happen to find a space with a walk-in cooler already in it—an old restaurant building, for instance—excellent. First, be sure it is a cooler and not a meat locker! You will want to spend the money to be sure the walk-in is in excellent working order. And be sure to have it professionally cleaned. You don't want your store or your flower arrangements to have any peculiar smells.

The chance of there being an existing walk-in in your leased space is slim, so the next thing on your list is to purchase one and have it installed. There are companies who are in the business of doing just that (Bush, for one; see Appendix for contact information). Pre-engineered walk-ins are designed for easy assembly and disassembly to be moved or expanded. So, don't feel pressure that you need to make the decision about this substantial investment that will carry you through your entire retail floral career!

There are thousands of different styles and designs. Your needs should be very basic. Walk-ins are typically in the noncustomer part of the store, easily accessible to your design table. Even if one wall is exposed in the retail section, it can be covered by a false wall or curtain. You could put the checkout counter in front of it and cover the walk-in wall with posters and other useful information. If your needs are for a large walk-in and your space is appropriate—for instance, in a small strip mall—you can consider a walk-in that attaches to the outside of the building. Of course, with this option your landlord will need to approve of the hole in the wall needed to access the walk-in from your shop.

Expect to pay a few thousand dollars for a walk-in cooler. You can investigate leasing one, especially if you think you will be moving your space within a couple years, at which time you will probably have different needs. And you can search around for used walk-ins as well. Some manufacturers have a revolving inventory of used walk-ins.

To be a wise walk-in consumer, look for energy efficiency and warranty information. Be sure there is a service rep nearby who can provide service in pretty short order. Flowers cannot spend very long outside the right temperature, so you need to have a service technician in your general area.

Your shop space will dictate the cooler size. Buy as large as you can fit in the space, keeping in mind how it also fits into your revenue projections and expected level of business. You need to be able to have enough inventory on hand to bring in the revenue your projections state. However, remember that perishable inventory is often available for delivery on a daily basis. Mary B. of Wyoming Floral forewarns that this balancing act is something you will become more proficient at as you gain experience.

Reach-In Cooler

Another vital purchase is a reach-in cooler. This smaller cooler is the one that sits on the retail floor, has glass doors in front, and allows you to reach in and take things out of it. They, too, come in a myriad of sizes, and you will have no problem finding just the right one for your shop. The reach-in cooler is a must—it brings flowers right to the retail customer, getting them in the mood for buying flowers by being able to look directly at an attractive display of different colors, different types of flowers, and different price ranges.

Consider your reach-in cooler an important shop display element and organize and decorate it accordingly. It typically has several adjustable shelves. Make sure to arrange cut flowers in attractive containers. Refresh the inventory at least daily, adding stems as well as weeding out less-than-fresh flowers. Be sure to have several arrangements in the cooler. If it is a holiday, have a few arrangements in the reach-in for those customers who are in a hurry and/or forgot to order arrangements for loved ones. Customers appreciate being able to buy a finished arrangement for a hostess gift or centerpiece for a dinner party without having to call ahead or wait for an arrangement to be created.

If your reach-in has the space, put in an arrangement or two waiting to be delivered or picked up. It is good advertising to show walk-in customers some finished products even if they aren't for sale. But don't crowd the reach-in so much that customers can't tell where one arrangement ends and the other begins.

Reach-in coolers can be bought with several different finishes such as black, white, stainless, or wood grain, to match your shop décor. They can also double as a walk-in, with the reach-in part in the front and the walk-in cooler behind the wall of the reach-in. This is a good compromise for a small shop with a space issue. It is also great for the larger shop—the main walk-in can serve as inventory storage and the attached reach-in cooler can provide storage for arrangements awaiting pickup or delivery.

Sink Area

Be sure to install a large utility sink in your work area. Make it as long and deep as space allows. Better yet, have a double sink with two different depths, but don't sacrifice sink size for the double sink. One large deep sink is better than two small ones, even if they are at differing depths.

You will want a flat area nearby or even as part of the sink that allows you to set cut flowers or vases down as you work. Whatever you do, don't underestimate the value of flat space in your work area.

As part of your plumbing/sink area, it would be helpful to have a dishwasher, the best way to get vases sparkling clean.

Arranging Table

You are going to need a large clear flat space to make arrangements and bouquets. Be sure the surface is water resistant. If you use a wood table, you might want to put a coat of paste wax or other water sealant on it. Have a raised table beside your work area that can hold wrapping paper for those cut flower bouquets without a vase. The raised table helps keep water away from the wrap.

Wrapping can be done at the checkout counter, but you run the risk of getting water droplets on the counter where customers write out gift enclosures, set greeting cards they want to purchase, or simply place their own personal belongings.

Checkout Counter

No matter how you design your shop, have a checkout area that is clearly marked. Don't make customer hunt to find the place where they pay. The checkout counter should, for the most part, be strictly for that purpose. It is a good place to put a few "impulse" items like small books, greeting cards, glass flowers, or dried flower bookmarks. But don't crowd the space so much that customers can't pay for their purchases without being afraid of knocking something off.

You must have a cash register, an important and relatively inexpensive item, on your checkout counter. Simple cash registers can be purchased at most office supply stores. If you want to integrate your cash register with inventory

---

Bright Idea

Keep a small notebook full of ideas for brief messages to write inside blank greeting cards—lines of poetry and other simple messages. Organize the notebook in "birthday greetings," "condolences," or "wedding messages." Better still, print them out from your computer onto small squares of vellum paper for customers to paste inside their blank greeting card purchase.

tracking and credit card sales, you will need to go with a computerized system. However, your start-up operation probably won't be large enough to warrant that for a while.

Don't make your checkout counter so tall that your average customers have to get on their tiptoes to hand you cash or write checks. Depending on your shop décor, you might use a large table for the checkout area. Just keep it clear, and especially when it is not as noticeable as a formal checkout counter, make some blunt indication that this is where you pay for your items. A sign hanging from the ceiling or on the front, or a wooden butler-like statue that says "checkout" or "pay for purchases here" works perfectly.

Other Furniture

No matter what your style, you will need to have some furnishings for display items. You want to have flat-top furnishings to display other kinds of floral accessories, such as dried and silk flowers and arrangements. And, to make your shop interesting and to add to sales, you want some sidelines, which often need very specific display furniture to show them off adequately. Other product lines just need something to set them on that fits into your shop's overall look.

Greeting Card Racks

Greeting cards are a great sideline in a florist's shop. Flowers are often purchased as gifts, and greeting cards often accompany gifts. Don't trap your card stock by buying lots of cards with preprinted messages. Some are nice, but it's better still to have an array of blank cards with images that are appropriate for the types of holidays and occasions that flowers are part of—funerals, birthdays, etc.

Greeting cards should be displayed in racks consisting of wire, wood, or Plexiglas made especially for cards. You should have no trouble finding the appropriate kind for your shop. Floor stand spinner racks hold lots of inventory and take up only a small footprint. Spinners are also available as countertop models. Wall racks use otherwise blank wall space and become decorative in themselves. Card companies often will include a display rack with a certain size order, especially to new customers.

Rotate your cards often and keep them out of direct sunlight or especially dusty areas; they can quickly become shopworn. And always ask customers if they need a card with their arrangements or bouquets—offer them free gift tags, of course, but also remind them that you have a lovely inventory of greeting cards that might be just right.

Bookshelves

Books can be appropriate to sell in almost any venue. Like card racks, their display shelves are available in an array of styles (floor, wall, countertop) and types (wood, Plexiglas, metal, painted). Some publishers of small gift book series also offer display racks at a certain purchase level.

Consider carrying books on flower care, especially if you sell plants such as orchids, African violets, or bonsai. Books on home design (that incorporate flowers) and gift books that would be appropriate to accompany wedding, birthday, or anniversary flowers are all good impulse items. Some can be displayed on the checkout counter, others can be displayed with an arrangement to plant the seed of how compatible the two items are.

Seating

No matter how small your shop, carving out an area where you can sit with clients is a good use of space. In order to be considered a good florist for wedding flowers, you need to be able to sit and listen to your clients discuss their wishes. Grieving family members who come to the shop to order funeral, gravesite, and casket flowers want to do it in some level of privacy. If these markets are ones on which you wish to hang your florist hat, it simply cannot be done adequately while standing at the checkout counter with other customers. If someone asks a friend where to go for wedding flowers, you want the friend to name your shop because "the florist sits down with you and really listens."

The seating area should be consistent with your overall shop décor—and should, of course, include plants and flowers. Use a freestanding mantle as a backdrop. Hang a floral still life above the mantle and set flowers and vases on the mantle. Include a coffee table in the area where you can display books and magazines to help customers communicate with you about the style they are looking for. This area can also be used

Tip...

Smart Tip
Anything that is not your core retail item—in this case flowers—is known as a "sideline." Be sure to carry a certain number of sidelines, usually small items that customers purchase on impulse and can expand sales. They can make your shop more interesting to look at and change your shop's appearance and keep it fresh for repeat customers.

Bright Idea

Just because trellises are intended to be outdoor garden furniture doesn't mean you can't use them effectively in your store. Trellises add a vertical dimension that helps break up the monotony of flat surfaces and let the customers' eyes travel all over the store rather than just focus on one plane.

by customers while they are waiting for you to finish with another customer. It can showcase your FTD or Teleflora books as well. The seating area is a nice touch and well worth the space.

Display Furniture

Your retail florist shop needs to be a lovely place to walk into. That means it can't consist of just a reach-in cooler full of flowers and a checkout counter. You will want to display dried flowers, silk flowers, perhaps some live plants, and other floral-related items—interesting vases and pitchers and other flower holders. Candles, candle holders, lavender or balsam sachets, anything to do with flowers, plants, and fragrances are appropriate retail items.

To add to the attractiveness of these items, display them interesting pieces of furniture. Perhaps the best thing to do (and the most fun) is to start shopping used furniture stores. Look for bureaus that have drawers that can provide storage as well as display space. Consider trellises to hang items like dried flowers and ornaments from. Lightweight latticework can be suspended from the ceiling. You can use it to hang pots, dried flowers, and other great sideline items.

Practical Matters

There are lots of other little things to think of when you are outfitting your store. In the bustle of getting coolers ordered and installed and figuring out the large-scale parts of outfitting a shop, it is critical to remember the seemingly little things—like adequate lighting and safe, resilient flooring.

Lighting

Install some permanent lighting, like recessed fixtures and track lighting with moveable fixtures, but don't go solely with immoveable light. Table lamps and floor lamps offer a nice atmosphere. Hopefully, windows will provide your shop with a lot of natural lighting during daylight hours. Be sure there is adequate lighting in your seating area to enable cus-

Stat Fact

From 1999 to 2010 there will be an 11 percent increase in the household population and a 15 percent increase in floral purchase transactions.

—American Floral Endowment research papers

tomers to easily look at magazines and books. Of course, the lighting in your work area behind the scenes should be ample, without causing glare to strain and tire your eyes.

Flooring

Depending on what kind of flooring exists in your retail space, use safe, rubber-backed throw rugs amply. Your shop can look more interesting if you can change the floor surface for different areas, but under no circumstances should you create different floor levels that could be a tripping hazard.

The Work Space

The space where you do most of the floral design and make arrangements should be set up with comfort in mind. Keep things within easy reach, allow for lots of flat surface to gather your materials before you start an arrangement, and have the sink easily accessible to the arranging area. Have a trash bin at subtable level that allows you to sweep stem trimmings, wire pieces, and other trash off the table and into the bin, making it easy to keep your workspace neat and clutter-free.

Don't forget the flooring in the work area. Use padding under rugs to create an area that is easy to stand on for several hours a day. Use a raised table or counter surface to arrange on standing up; have a couple of comfortable barstools handy so you can sit when you feel like it. Learn about body mechanics, and make yourself comfortable during the long retail day.

> ### Beware!
> Retail shop owners should always be on the lookout for potential hazards that could cause customers to get hurt and sue. Throw rugs should have non-skid backing and lay flat on the floor. Be very wary of renting a space that has a raised area in the retail area where customers have to notice that they need to step up or down. This is an accident waiting to happen. Any time you see someone trip or stumble into something, don't wait for it to be a bigger deal; lessen the hazard as soon as possible.

Flowers, Flowers, Wherefore Art Thou?

 retail business needs to have suppliers to stock its stores. You need to use the best suppliers you can find that deliver high-quality merchandise in your required timeframe and at a cost that allows you to make a profit.

▲

Finding Suppliers

Mary B. of Wyoming Florists advocates buying as much of your flower inventory locally as you possibly can. There are many places you can order online and over the phone, and shipping is pretty easy. Still, she wants someone she can go to when there is a problem. Having a strong relationship with a local vendor also gives you a source willing to go the extra mile for you if you need inventory quickly for an unexpected job.

If you start work on filling an order and find a shipment of the flowers is bad, the local vendor can more likely remedy the problem immediately. When the unexpected big job comes in, the local vendor is not going to be willing to drop everything and get you what you need when you usually order from an online vendor.

Bright Idea

When looking for your flower suppliers, choose vendors who offer more than meets the eye. For example, Bay State Florist in New Hampshire has staff members who are former floral designers. They can sit down with new shops owners and help them be successful. Don't be afraid to ask your supplier for help like this—it is to its advantage that you are successful so your shop will be around to buy its flowers, and perhaps expand into an even larger customer!

Most areas of the United States have flower wholesalers. For instance, in New Hampshire, Bay State Florist Supply is one of several suppliers in the area. A full-service florist wholesaler, Bay State brings in flowers from growers all over the world thus offering florists in the region access to all the flowers they might need. Bay State also has a complete "hard goods" department, providing vases, silk flowers, and all manner of the nonflower supplies. And if that isn't enough, it also has a greenhouse arm that provides its customers with live plants.

Bay State hears from its florist customers almost daily and does its own deliveries so customers are not only getting the freshest flowers possible, but they are also dealing directly with the company on all levels.

Smart Tip

Tip...

In business, relationships are the name of the game. Treat your vendors with respect and use them wisely. Develop a relationship with several vendors. Although you should expect excellent service and excellent product, remember that without vendors you would have nothing to sell.

What do wholesalers spend a lot of time doing? Checking and doublechecking the orders they receive before they send them along to their customers—so what you, the florist, gets are the highest quality flowers available.

A local supplier with whom you can build an ongoing relationship is critical to any retail florist's success. You also don't want to put all your eggs in one basket, so having a few suppliers with whom you establish strong relationships is critical.

Establishing Accounts

Typically your initial inventory will be part of your start-up expenses, unless perhaps you have credit history from another retail shop you have owed. Whether flowers or not, most companies will establish an account with a small credit limit after you pay cash for your first order.

Once your shop is up and running and you have a few accounts you've ordered from and paid (on time, of course), other new accounts you want to open may start offering you small lines of credit right up front.

And once you have established yourself with your accounts, they will increase your credit limit, enabling you to expand your sales. Remember, by requiring initial upfront payment, they are just safeguarding their own businesses. Wholesalers very much want to help you succeed; your success means additional business for them.

Online Sources

While you'll want to develop strong relationships with local wholesalers and get most of your products from them, you can expand your supply sources by buying directly from many growers by phone or via the internet and their web sites. Experiment with a few, but always be sure you are dealing with a reputable company. Look for affiliations with American or international floral associations, and check them out at florist's conventions. A couple of growers to investigate are:

- Ocean View Flowers, www.oceanview flowers.com; (800) 736-5608. This California grower specializes in "premium fresh cut flowers," especially stock, larkspur, and delphinium.
- FloraTrading, www.floratrading.com. Buy roses, tropicals, and filler flowers directly

Beware!
Don't always choose suppliers and inventory based on cost. While cost is a significant factor in how much profit you make, you don't want to choose low cost at the expense of quality and timely delivery. If you don't have flowers or the flowers are of poor quality and don't last, you won't have orders and customers anyway.

from Ecuador, picked to your order, and delivered in three days by UPS.

- AgroTropical, www.agrotropical.andes.com. Order roses wholesale from Colombia and Ecuador.

There are many, many others. Search online and check out their web sites to find out more.

Common Flowers and Their Care

Perishable is the name of the florist game. One of the most basic things you need to learn as quickly as possible is how to care for your stock. It all starts with your wholesalers and suppliers—pick the most reputable ones to deal with and get the best flowers you can. Your suppliers are also your best source of information on care. Read the information they provide, and don't hesitate to call them when you are in doubt.

Following are some general tips on the most common flowers in basic arrangements. Flowers aren't all quite as delicate as you might think, but they all do require the right care.

Tip...

Smart Tip

Michelle of Bay State Florists in New Hampshire emphasizes the importance of developing strong relationships between retailers and suppliers, as well as among retailers themselves. She recommends joining local chapters of the national florist societies, attending meetings, and being very involved in the community. She says, "When everyone sticks together, they can help each other out. When the economy is bad, for instance, they can find out from each other what is working and what is not."

Going Up?

"**M**ark up" refers to how much you can charge for items over and above what you paid for them. If a dozen roses cost you $5 and you can sell them for $20, you have a 4 times markup. How much you can mark things up depends a lot on the area you are selling in. You need to make money on your sales to be profitable. So if the highest quality roses mean you can only mark them up a couple of bucks because that is all your market will bear, you need to find ways to get those roses cheaper. Either look for a lesser (but not poor!) quality supplier that will satisfy your customers, or do things like buying in larger quantities to get lower overall prices.

Bacteria Control

Bacteria is the enemy of the cut flower. The little packets that come with most bouquets are preservatives that help prevent the growth of bacteria in the water in which the cut flowers sit. The bacteria causes premature wilting. In order to keep them in check, you must also keep your containers and any utensils like scissors—clean and disinfected. Some plants also will need a spray-on preservative.

Hydration

Some flowers will be delivered in water; some will be delivered dry and require you to hydrate them using solutions like Quick Dip. The preparation of flowers in your shop is known as "processing." This involves removing them from boxes, undoing their ties when necessary, cutting stems, removing any petals that will fall below the water line, hydration in the case of dry shipping, and generally getting the flowers either in the walk-in or reach-in cooler and ready for sale. Customers should also be instructed to re-cut most flowers before putting them in their vase at home and again a few days after they receive/purchase them.

Nutrients

Like any living thing, flowers need nutrients. The pH level for cut flowers should be three to four. Preservative packets also typically contain nutrients such as sugar and a germicide to extend cut flowers life. You can buy these nutrients/preservatives in bulk for use in the shop and in packets for distribution to customers with their purchases.

Lifespans

The desires of the customer will of course be your main concern when choosing flowers for an arrangement. But many customers won't choose specific flowers and you will instead want to consider the lifespan and care requirements of the flowers you put in an arrangement. Following is some basic information about common cut flowers.

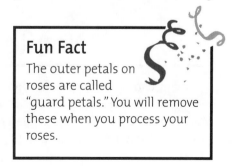

Fun Fact

The outer petals on roses are called "guard petals." You will remove these when you process your roses.

- *Roses.* Roses tend to have a vase life of a week or less. They do need their stems cut before placing in water.

- *Carnations.* Carnations come grown in several colors and can be dyed almost any color, making them a popular choice for decorating. They are hardy flowers and can be displayed in water out on the retail floor (although it is best to put them in the cooler overnight). They have a long vase life of one to two weeks.

- *Liatris.* This is a basic flower that is used to add dimension to an arrangement or bouquet. They last in water for a couple of weeks.

- *Lilies.* Lilies are hardy, lasting for a couple of weeks. They can be out on the sales floor during the day. They should have their stems re-cut every three to four days.

Smart Tip

Mary B. of Wyoming Florists admits that the perishable aspect is the most difficult part of the florist business. Her two main pieces of advice are "don't over-order and be careful to rotate your stock." And she says not to worry, experience will eventually allow you to be pretty good at ordering accurately and avoiding waste.

- *Freesia.* Freesia is a delicate-looking, very fragrant flower. They typically last less than a week.

- *Fillers.* There are several ferns and other light flowers such as baby's breath that are commonly used to fill out a bouquet and add dimension and a good backdrop to show off the colorful flowers. You'll always want to have a supply on hand.

- *Tropicals.* Tropical flowers refer, logically, to those that live in tropical environments. Some common cut species include Bird of Paradise, Heliconia, and Anthurium. Tropicals typically should be kept in a temperature no lower than 55 degrees.

- *Dutch flowers.* The rather delicate but popular group of flowers that come from Holland are the classic tulips, daffodils, narcissus, iris, and anemones.

- *Exotics.* Orchids are perhaps the most popular exotic. If you learn a lot about orchids, you can develop a whole sideline around them because they are commonly collected, and collectors are always looking for new types to add to their collections.

Nonflower Supplies

If you choose a supplier for your flowers like Bay State in New Hampshire, you will get a full-service supplier for all your needs beyond just cut flowers and live plants. You can find suppliers from whom you can also get your vases and other hard goods, or you can look for separate suppliers. It is probably best to do both.

Look through the floral trade magazines (see Appendix) to find suppliers for things like rose boxes (Gift Box Corporation of America and Signature Design Boxes are just a couple) and ribbons. And look outside the floral industry to find unusual supplies that will make your store unique. Don't be afraid to use supplies that are not designed specifically for use with flowers; it can be a signature touch.

The basic nonflower supplies you need for your start-up include:

- foam
- scissors and shears
- moss
- glue and glue guns
- wire
- boxes
- plastic wrap for bouquets
- outer wrap for bouquets
- vases
- other containers for arrangements
- containers for holding flowers in coolers
- wire for stiffening flowers
- spray, bulk, and packets of preservative
- ribbon
- gift tags
- cleaning products
- wreath forms
- delivery trays for your delivery vehicle(s)
- decorative doodads

Beware!

The flower industry is not immune to scam artists. On its web site at the time of this writing, Gold Medallion Florist Network warned customers that someone was calling its members claiming to be "Gold Medallion Flora" and getting customers to renew their memberships. When the real Gold Medallion called to get members to renew, many members thought they had already renewed, and their credit cards were charged several times by the false organization. Beware of scams. Don't think that just because you're dealing with pretty flowers it can't happen.

9

Helpful Professional Credentials and Training

Becoming a florist does not require expensive formal training. There are many opportunities to learn the craft through coursework, but the most common way people learn about being a florist is the old fashioned way—through apprenticing and on-the-job training.

Work in the Business

Any time you consider starting a business in any field, it is wise to work in the industry for a while before going out on your own. If you are planning to start your own business soon in a competing market or category, you should be up front with your prospective employer. Although many will be wary and not want to hire a future competitor, others will see a couple of classic advantages to allowing someone to apprentice:

- The employee who is looking to learn the profession will probably be a more dedicated staff member than the person who is just looking for a way to get a paycheck.
- Your potential employer could see this as a possible expansion opportunity (when you are ready to open your business, you might be able to open a satellite store in a different community) or as a possible way for her to retire by having you eventually buy her out.

The shop you choose to apprentice in does not have to be exactly like the shop you intend to open. In fact, being different may be better—you can learn a lot about what you want to do by learning what you don't want to do. Perhaps you choose to work at an upscale florist in a wealthy neighborhood. But what you find is that you want to spend your day in a more down-to-earth, less fancy environment fulfilling orders for people for whom buying a bouquet is a small investment. This is a good thing to learn before you open shop and surround yourself with roses and special tropicals in high-style vases only to find that you would rather be designing carnation bouquets in country pitchers. But what you learn in the more trendy shop can be of great benefit eventually by giving your traditional arrangements a unique slant.

> **Beware!**
> Do not use apprenticing as a way to learn trade secrets of competing businesses. This is simply unethical and not the way you want to do business. Look for a job in a market some distance away from the key market you plan to tap into with your future shop. And always be up front with your employer about your plans.

Try Everything

When you do land a job at a florist, don't limit yourself to doing only the part you really think you like—designing, ordering, making arrangements, talking with customers. Do it all. Ask your employer to let you try your hand at everything from stocking shelves, doing deliveries, caring for the flowers, cleaning the walk-in unit, and designing and building a window display.

When you own your own business, you need to know how to do everything that needs to be done to keep the business going. Of course, you can choose to hire employees who do most of the walk-in cleaning and the shelf stocking, but employees are never as reliable as the owner. It is important to know all the jobs your shop entails. Plus that way, you know the problems your employees might encounter and can be supportive when they request certain cleaners to help clean the walk-in or a hands-free phone unit to take orders with.

College-Bound

If you want formal training in the florist business, there are certainly ways to get it. Formal training is mostly in the form of community college programs. Some examples are:

- *South Florida School of Floral Design*, 1612 South Dixie Highway, Lake Worth, FL 33460, (561) 585-9491). This course is broken up into three 35-hour "phases" over three weeks, including Fresh Flower Arranging, Wedding Designs, and Funeral Designs, with each week including basic information on plant and flower care, mechanics, pricing, fertilization, and inventory control.

- *Floral Design Institute*, one site in Portland, Oregon, and one in Seattle, Washington. Check its web site at www.floraldesigninstitute.com. Established in 1969, this school offers programs ranging from those suitable for people just looking to arrange flowers for themselves to someone interested in opening his own florist shop. It also has a distance learning component.

- *Palmer School of Floral Design*, Palmer Design Center, 3710 Mitchell Drive, Fort Collins, Colorado 80525, (970) 207-9476, www.palmerschooloffloraldesign.com. This school was started in 2001 by the owners of Palmer Flowers, the recipient of the 2005 Florist of the Year award. To complete its certification program, you take four 30-hour courses that cover the complete range of topics in floral design. Total tuition is around $1,500.

This is just a short list of formal florist design programs in the United States. Search online and check the web sites of the state and national floral associations (see the Appendix for a list) for many more.

Smart Tip

Tip...

Mary B., owner of Wyoming Florists in Wyoming, Ohio, put in 16 years working side-by-side with her in-laws with the intention of buying them out at their retirement. She enjoyed getting so close to her in-laws, but if she had it to do over, she says one thing she would do differently is have "gotten more active earlier in the business when my in-laws still owned it." Mary realized how much she had learned when in the first year she took over the main responsibility for the shop, in the transition period of buying her in-laws out, she doubled the shop's take-home revenue.

Online

There are floral certification programs that can be completed online. Check out Career Choice Wizard (www.careerchoicewizard.com) and its certificate program in floral design, which is accredited by The Accrediting Council of Independent Colleges and Schools, Accrediting Commission of the Distance Education and Training Council (DETC). This program does not educate you in opening your own business, if that is already a strength and you want to learn the florist end of the retail industry, this program may be a convenient way to get some credentials. There are other online programs such as the PCDI Home Study courses at www.career-courses.net, so shop around a for one that suits your interests, price range, and credibility level.

Continuing Education

Even after you have gone through a floral design program, plan to take a few classes here and there to keep up with the trends in the industry. Probably the best way to do that is to take time out of your busy retail life and make sure to attend at least one annual national floral convention each year (check all the association web sites frequently for upcoming conventions). These conventions and trade shows are an education in themselves—exhibits and booths will give you a good sense of what the trends are and what is happening in other parts of the country that may hit your region eventually.

Beyond the information you can gain just by walking around the show floor, trade conventions also typically offer a dizzying array of seminars and classes. And often they are at no cost beyond the original cost of admission. Take full advantage of these conventions. The organizations that put them on know exactly the kinds of things you need to know and learn, and they make the best use of your time. And besides, they are usually located in fun and interesting cities and give you the chance to network with florists from all over the country and beyond.

Smart Tip

Tip...

Retailers often get so caught up in the day-to-day workings of their shops that they feel like getting away for a trade conference is just not possible. Do not fall into that trap. Getting away from the shop is a good thing to do. Going to a trade show in your industry can be invigorating and go a long way to helping prevent burnout. You will bring home ideas and contacts that make up for any time away from the shop.

Is It Worth It?

To make a floral design program a worthwhile expenditure of your time and money, you need to

Fun Fact

The techniques of wiring, using floral foam, tying bouquets—basically how to keep things together—is known as "mechanics." You don't want your arrangements falling apart, especially since they need to survive being transported. Mary B. of Wyoming Florists advises becoming proficient in this area, "If you learn good mechanics, a lot of the rest is just a matter of interpretation."

get a return on your investment. If you were looking to get a job as a florist in a shop owned by someone else, a certificate in floral design might earn you a dollar or two more an hour in salary. However, its more practical advantage may be to get you a job faster.

As for the logic of a certificate program, if you plan to start your own retail florist shop, there are some credibility advantages to being able to put "graduate of blah blah blah" and perhaps a few letters after your name. This is especially true if you are opening your shop in an area where you are completely unknown. The advantage dwindles in your hometown or a town where you have lived for many years and raised your children. People there will remember how you always had an interest in flowers or a way with crafts and will try you out based on their personal knowledge. Whether they come back for repeat business will then rely solely on their experience the first time, not whether you are credentialed in any way.

Learning About a Niche

Most retail florists shops need to find a niche market to boost their revenues. The wedding market is perhaps the most lucrative of those niches. In order to become proficient and known in the market, however, you must learn the tricks of the trade. Go to bridal shows and florists' conventions where the wedding market is often a big focus. Exhibit at local bridal shows to get your name out there; these shows are very well attended by brides-to-be looking for the professionals who will create their weddings. Subscribe to (and read) bridal magazines (*Brides, Modern Bride, Elegant Bride, Weddings*, just to name a few), and find out what the trends are in the wedding world. There are some traditions that just don't change, but each year brings new fads and ideas.

You need to know what you are talking about when you talk with brides and grooms and other family members involved in the wedding planning. The language isn't complicated, but you can't forget the checklist of wedding flowers that need to be planned, including corsages, boutonnieres, flower petals, and, of course, the bride's bouquet. You need to help the bridal party understand how to use these and why the bouquet, if it is going to be tossed, needs to be sturdily tied. These are the things that will make them feel confident in your ability to help make their weddings a special day.

Other Credentials

There are a few other credentials you may need, depending on your business.

Commercial License

You certainly need a driver's license for almost any delivery business, but, if you decide to have a large refrigerated delivery truck, you may also need a commercial driver's license. The Commercial Motor Vehicle Safety Act of 1986 brought safety standards that are the same for all states. You need a commercial license if your delivery vehicle has a manufacturer's gross vehicle weight rating (GVWR) of over 26,000 pounds. This is a pretty large vehicle, and you probably wouldn't use this for day-to-day deliveries. But

The Color Wheel

Anyone involved in design of any kind needs to become familiar with the color wheel. There are many good web sites, books, and even software programs that make this something that should be easy to do.

Color theory is described by The Color Wheel Pro as a "set of principles used to create harmonious color combinations." The color wheel visually represents color theory. It is not new science—Sir Isaac Newton actually "created" the color wheel in 1666 to show how light is graded into the spectrum of color.

Not only is this good to use with your floral creations, but you will want to use color theory and the color wheel in the layout and design of your shop, including window and other displays.

But color theory is not only used in creating color schemes that are pleasing to the eye. Different colors have different effects on mood as well, a theory put forth by Johann Wolfgang von Goethe, who created a color wheel that showed psychological effects of color—blue is cooling, yellow is warming. Some colors create excitement, and others enhance mellow moods.

You don't have to go to school to learn about color theory, but if you do take florist classes (or almost any art class), you will certainly explore the color wheel in depth.

refrigeration adds a lot of weight to a vehicle, so know the rules and follow them. Check with your state motor vehicle division to learn how to obtain a commercial license.

Hazardous Waste Handling

Unless you choose to operate a cut flower farm large enough to supply florists, you probably won't use enough pesticides and insecticides to require you to be licensed, but you should know the laws. You also need to understand how to safely dispose of empty hazardous waste containers in your community. Do not be cavalier about these kinds of things—not only is it the law but it is the law because it is environmentally unsafe to simply throw some things in the trash. You do not want your business name in the papers for violating environmental laws.

Tricks of the Trade

Not everything, of course, must be learned in a flower shop. Information in some areas—security or customer services, for example—can be learned anywhere. You may already have learned some retail tricks of the trade in a retail job in the past. If not, here are some things to think about.

- *Don't underestimate the need for security*. If you're selling refrigerators, petty theft will not be a problem. But any retail shop that has small items that are easy to pocket is a target for shoplifters. The size of your shop will have a bearing on how substantial a security system you need, but even the smallest shop should have one or two well-placed mirrors to deter shoplifting.

- *Most liability insurance holders send you some information along with the policy to help you avoid liability situations*. If someone trips and falls in your store, for example, your insurance will advise you to be helpful and polite but never apologize—this implies that you are guilty of something. For example, if they tripped over a box on the shop floor don't say, "I'm so sorry. I never should have left that box there." If the case were to go to court, lawyers will make a run for it using those kinds of comments.

- *Learn about traffic patterns and good shop design*. A lot will depend on the size and configuration of your store. Look around in some of the big retailers to see how they do it. Retail trade magazines can be expensive, but perhaps you can share a subscription with someone or borrow some back issues. This is where you need to understand the color wheel and how to draw people into your store and to carry them through the whole store, not just in a small area near the door.

- *Customer service on the retail floor is also a fine art.* Learn the balance between ignoring someone and pestering them—no shopper likes either. And when someone does want your help, you want to learn the nuances of tipping them into a sale instead of having them walk out the door empty handed.
- *Lastly, learn window and in-store display techniques.* These are great selling tools. If you have any artistic flair, you will probably do fine. If you don't, look for someone who does, when you hire employees. Or find a college art student and hire her to come in and change your window and floor displays. And do this on a regular basis—at least a couple times a month—to encourage shoppers to come back to your store time and again because every time it looks new.

If this is news to you, the best way to learn it all is to work in a retail environment before opening your store. Do this in a well-established, successful store. You will pick up the best knowledge of what to do and what not to do.

A Rose by Any
Other Name

Marketing and promoting any business is critical. If no one knows you exist, you won't get many customers. The average customer will probably only order a few bouquets and arrangements per year—you will need lots of those customers to reach even modest revenue goals. Marketing helps those customers find you.

A rule of thumb in advertising is that people need to hear and see something three times for it to really register and be remembered. So think outside of the box when it comes to marketing and advertising your business. For instance, say Jill goes to the grocery store and sees your flier on the bulletin board. A couple of days later, she is having breakfast with a couple friends and she sees your business card ad on the restaurant's placemat. That evening, she is reading the paper and sees a press release that you, owner of Flo's Floral, are giving a talk at the local library later that month. The following week, Jill talks to a friend whom she hasn't seen in a while and finds out that her friend's birthday is next week—and it is the big 5-0! Guess who Jill is going to call to order flowers for her friend? Just by being there, you have a new customer.

Marketing Plan

Before you even get to the actual marketing, it is wise to have a plan. Things you will want to consider in your marketing plan include

- a selection of printed materials and a list of places to distribute them,
- paid advertising,
- well-timed press releases,
- online marketing, and
- other marketing vehicles such as speaking engagements or volunteer work.

Printed Materials

Any business can benefit from marketing materials such as press releases, business cards, and brochures. But don't just create printed materials and stick them on a shelf somewhere to collect dust—use them. Don't just send out one press release and then stop. Keep at it.

Press Releases

A press release is a piece of information released in a timely fashion to media outlets who might use it in various ways. A newspaper may run your press release as filler in the paper, or they may find it of enough interest to call you and do a separate story on you or your business.

Send press releases to every newspaper and radio in your market range. Find out names of editors to send them to; don't just send them blind. And send them to several editors—the business editor, the lifestyle editor, the news desk, the Sunday edition editor.

Start-up is a great time to get free publicity through press releases. Write them so that the most important or intriguing information comes first, enticing the editor to read on and to think about where this might fit in her paper.

Press releases can be appropriate at other times as well:

- Before Valentine's Day, create a short press release on how to care for a bouquet of roses.
- Keep tabs on research and studies, such as how receiving a bouquet from a husband has been shown to be important to a healthy relationship!
- Announce your graduation from some professional florist certification program, or perhaps an award you, your shop, or your main designer has received.

Business Cards

Business cards are so cheap and easy to print these days, there's no reason not to have a generous supply on hand at all times. Don't print them on your own computer, use a quick printing service, and get a box of 1,000 printed.

Be sure your business card is simple, easy to read, and contains all your pertinent business information (store name, address, phone, fax, and web site address if you have one) while not being too crowded. And have your card designed to reflect your shop's style. If you have a slant toward country style, a single red rose on a black business card with gold printing suggests something quite different.

If you have a specialty, come up with a one-line slogan and print it on your business card and all other marketing materials.

Keep a supply of business cards with you at all times. Give them to your staff. Unless your shop is quite large, your staff may not need personalized cards, but they can use a generic card and write their names on it when necessary.

Pick up a few business card holders and place them strategically around your shop. Always put one stack beside the checkout area. Whenever you speak with anyone about anything that may have some follow-up potential, hand them a business card. You would be surprised when it might pop up as the perfect solution to where to get an arrangement made.

Post business cards on bulletin boards where appropriate—the local breakfast spot, for instance, often has a place for business cards. If your card has enough information on it, place it in publications with "business card sections" for advertising.

Slogans

A marketing slogan can be a useful tool. Although you certainly don't need to spend half your marketing budget hiring the advertising agency that did all the branding for

Coca-Cola, you also don't want to bother with a slogan that states the obvious (e.g., "fresh flowers for sale"). But if your shop has a significant specialty, you pride yourself in some aspect of customer service, you have a nationally known designer on staff, or you have a van that does house calls to discuss wedding plans, that could provoke a useful slogan.

If you do come up with a slogan, use it everywhere—your business card, your brochures, your other printed marketing materials, your web site, on the side of your delivery van, and even on your phone message and at the top of your invoices and sales receipts.

Brochures

Brochures can help provide customers with information that will move them from thinking about ordering to actually placing an order. Sometimes, you just need to tap their imaginations.

You can also create informational brochures—how to care for the top ten cut flowers, for example—that may be kept around longer. Print your business information or even a replica of your business card at the top. Check with the floral trade associations—some trade organizations provide generic brochures that you can purchase for a modest fee and staple your business card to the top.

If your shop specializes in weddings or another niche, a brochure that fully outlines your experience and why your shop is the best for wedding flowers can help brides-to-be have a take-home piece to refer to later as they finalize their wedding suppliers.

And by all means, if you or someone on your staff has special credentials, experience, or awards, your marketing brochure is the place to flaunt that.

Paid Advertising

A regular paid ad in a well-chosen newspaper is probably a good idea for any retail store. But don't just insert an ad here and there. Come up with an affordable ad size, and stick with it—run it every Thursday or every Saturday morning or every Monday and Friday. For the ad to be effective, it has to be there regularly.

If you don't have an ad done and can't do it yourself, typically the paper will create one for you. Be sure to proofread it before it is printed—newspapers are notorious for typos; it is the nature of the fast-paced business they are in. And proofread the ad again each time you change something.

Some of the best papers to advertise in are the free weeklies. Their ad rates are usually very affordable, and they automatically make your ad a regular thing.

Smart Tip

Tip...

Paid advertising can be a money sucker. Good ad salespeople can readily make you think your sales will sky-rocket if you advertise in their newspapers (or tank if you don't). If you decide to spend money on paid newspaper ads, use a method that helps you track response. Coupon clipping and other specials related only to that ad can be good ways to do that.

Also, it is worth paying to have your business listed in the Yellow Pages in a display format. They are looked at more often than the two-line listings buried in the midst of all the other businesses that chose to buy display ads.

The Web Site

These days you really can't afford not to have a presence on the web. People who take pride in not having entered the electronic age are simply losing lots of potential business!

Your web site should list all the key information that of your marketing materials include. (Don't forget your slogan!) You can also add some drop down features such as a list of the kinds of flowers you stock, what sidelines you carry, or even a price list of some basic arrangements or bouquets. Go into a little detail about any specialty niche you service. Show the different funeral arrangements. Be informative while reminding viewers that you can fulfill their floral needs with top-notch service.

You can keep your web site simple to keep the costs down. If you don't use it for actual purchasing, you can get by with a small fee to host the site and have it updated monthly.

Signage

If no one knows what your store is offering, they probably won't be inclined to stop. Storefront signage is critical! It should not only indicate that you are a floral shop, but the sign design should be in the same style as your shop—elegant, fun, country. Whatever theme you choose for your shop, all of your signage should give the same image.

The size and style of the sign outside your store will depend a lot on its location. If you are in a strip mall, you will want the sign large enough for people driving by to read. A downtown store sign doesn't need to be quite as large as drivers will be able to get a tad closer. A downtown shop front will probably have some space restrictions because downtown buildings usually have small amounts of flat space to work with.

In all cases, light your sign. Even if you are never open after dark, you will want people going by to notice that there is a flower shop in your location.

Vehicle Signage

Even if you use a delivery service, you will probably do some amount of local delivery yourself. Be sure your van has signage—driving around with a moving ad provides great awareness of your business. And these days, magnetic vehicle signage is not expensive.

Association Memberships/Web Site Links and Searches

Membership in local associations—the chamber of commerce, small business groups like Business Networking International, gardening clubs—will not only provide you with some great ideas and moral support, but also customers. Bring a stack of business cards to every meeting and don't leave until everyone has one in hand.

Be judicious in your expenditure of memberships in national associations. Although dues are often modest, be sure the association is worth all the extra mail and e-mail it will generate. Choose ones that have local chapters that you can participate in. Many associations offer links to your web site that can be worth the dues.

Link up with other web sites as well. Often times you can get a link on a web site for a simple exchange—they can link on your web site and you on theirs. If there is an organization that puts together the local bridal show, get a link on its web site. Almost all funeral homes now have sophisticated web sites that offer links to services helpful to grieving families and friends who wish to show their sympathy.

Talk with large local companies who might have intranet sites—web sites designed strictly for company employees. Having a link on a site that reaches a large number of local people is a good thing to do.

Newsletters

Newsletters can be great marketing tools, but keep them simple and useful. You can make newsletters so complicated and comprehensive that they suck your time. Provide your customers with important information such as:

- *Your store hours.* Let customers know any vacations you have scheduled if your store

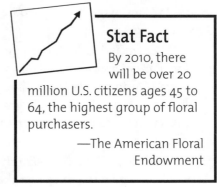

Stat Fact

By 2010, there will be over 20 million U.S. citizens ages 45 to 64, the highest group of floral purchasers.

—The American Floral Endowment

will be closed for an extended time, or if you are going to be closed for renovations or inventory. Also note if your hours change with the seasons.

- *Reminders of upcoming holidays.* Send your newsletter out to time it with a reminder to order Valentine's flowers or the table centerpiece for Thanksgiving.

- *Tips for flower care.* If you sell live plants, offer some tips on how to care for them. This can tempt people who don't have an orchid to take care of to come in and buy one.

- *Coupons.* Always offer some kind of incentive to get customers to come in to your shop, such as discount coupons that are good for the time span of the newsletter (a month) or if they order Valentine's flowers before the 7th of February.

Flower Talk

Giving seminars on plant care, flower arranging, or gardening at local garden clubs or community college noncredit programs can be time consuming, but it can also be a fun way to market your business. Sometimes you can make money at it, too.

And don't forget, the class may only be ten people at a time, but those ten people know a lot more people. Be sure they go home with your business cards to hand out to their friends and families.

Being a speaker can also give you additional credentials that you can add to your resume and brochure material. Be sure to get out a press release about any speaking engagements—another opportunity to get your business mentioned.

> **Tip...**
>
> **Smart Tip**
> If you like to write, are good with deadlines, and can fit in the time, approach the local weekly about writing a floral-related weekly column for the paper. This is a great way to get your business name in front of your target market.

Going the Extra Mile

Thinking up some creative ways to help your business stand out from the crowd can be a great marketing tactic—it gets people talking about your business. And your customers are your best form of advertisement.

Try things like:

- Have a list of suggestions for what to write on gift cards. People are often at a loss for words when it comes to writing a card, especially when they need to do it while they are standing at the counter. Handing them a list with ideas of lines appropriate for a birthday, funeral, or anniversary is an added-value feature your store can offer.

- Use up aging inventory by giving a free flower to the first six customers of the day. Put it in a little water holder so it will last a couple of days. They can put them on their desks in their offices and tell people where they got them. (Give them a couple business cards, of course.)

Have a suggestion box in the back room where your employees can come up with other ideas.

Customer
Service

Customer service is the key to most businesses, and a successful florist business is no exception. Whether it is retail or wholesale, repeat customers are essential. If you don't listen to your retail customers' needs or you don't stand by your floral products as a wholesaler, customers will simply go somewhere else. There is always another store or wholesaler to do business with.

What Do Customers Want?

The retail florist needs to address several customer needs. Customers expect you to deliver the quality you promise—from vases and trim to the flowers themselves. They expect you to do what you say when you say you will do it, especially when it comes to delivery of arrangements. They also, among other things, expect you to be open during the hours you advertise—how many of us have run to that little shop on the corner when we had an extra ten minutes only to find one of those little clocks on the door that indicates the shop owner will be back in 15 minutes. Sorry, lost not only that sale but that customer as well and probably a few of his friends and relatives! Here are some additional things to think about when it comes to providing the best customer service.

Quality

Customers come to your shop because of a promise you made, either through your promotional materials, your window display, or whatever they saw that brought them in. To keep those people as regular customers, you need to fulfill that promise of a quality arrangement. The flowers they see and the ones that get delivered to recipients need to be of the highest quality. The arrangement needs to be interesting and appropriate. It probably also needs to be good value, although that is remarkably less important than most people think. What you are striving for is for the recipient to tell the giver how lovely the arrangement was and what joy she got in receiving it. If the customer is going to see the arrangement, for instance at a funeral or at the family Christmas table, it needs to be exactly what she ordered, and then some. This will bring that customer to you again.

Reliability

Some portion of your retail business will be customers walking in the door and going away with a bouquet of cut flowers. But a large percentage of your business will be telephone orders delivered to a person other than the customer who called. The customer will need to expect you to be very reliable.

Don't make promises you may not be able to keep. If a customer needs an arrangement delivered the next day by noon, steer him away from unique flowers that require special ordering. Even if you think you can have the particular flower by the end of the business day, it is a fine line to get it. Make an interesting arrangement, and get it delivered in 24 hours or less, especially if you are a one-person shop. Encourage the customer to choose more common flowers and assure him that you can still make a unique and appropriate arrangement.

Delivery is a huge part of the retail florist business. Make sure you are clear about your delivery policy in your literature, on your web site, and in your voice mail message. Two day's notice? Twenty-four hours? A lot will depend on your delivery capabilities. If you are a one-person shop, you will need to keep it to a very practical level.

Even a funeral, while perhaps the least planned of all occasions calling for flowers, allows for at least 24 hours' notice, so don't feel like you have to shut your shop down several times a day to deliver flowers. Don't set your customers up for disappointment. And bend the rules a little for regular customers. They are your bread and butter, and sometimes they just don't call 48 hours ahead of time.

And when you give a delivery time, fulfill it. If it's appropriate to be early, do so. This is one place where you can go above and beyond the call of duty and earn very good favor with your customers.

Regularity

This is a subset of "reliability." If you start a retail store, set your business hours and keep them. You can certainly reduce hours on the off-season or, if you can't afford a part-time employee yet, close every day between noon and two for lunch and deliveries. But don't close between noon and two o'clock just when you feel like it—either do it every day and or only in real emergencies. Customers do not like to go out of their way to stop by your shop and find you closed during what they would assume to be normal business hours. They simply will take their business elsewhere. Pick your hours, display them on the shop door, on your mailing pieces, on your web site, and announce them on your answering machine message.

Presentation

Presentation can refer to the floral arrangements you create. However, your retail shop's presentation is critical as well. Present your store accurately. The outside should reflect what the customer is going to see when she comes inside. Of course, if your storefront is in disrepair, this is not going to attract many walk-in customers. Oh, there is always the exception to that, the town that has its "eccentric" shop owner, where you tell visiting friends and relatives that even though the place looks like a dump, it is well worth the visit. Don't be that shop owner. It is definitely the exception, not the rule, that a shop with a dumpy appearance is successful.

Use your signage and your window displays to reflect what you want your customers to know about your shop. Is it upscale? Is it more down-to-earth? Do you focus on organic flowers and environmentally friendly products? Is your focus as a florist more minimalist in style, like the Japanese approach to flower arranging? Let your customers know before they walk in the door if your shop is right for them. This is the beginning of making a good first impression.

Personal Touches

Most customers appreciate doing business with someone who remembers their purchasing habits. Keep a simple database of your customers and their purchases. If they will reveal their birthdate to you, send them a postcard for 20 percent off or a free flower on their birthday. If they sent a bouquet on Mother's Day, note that and send them a reminder to get their order in early during the busy season.

Another personal touch you can make is to read the obituaries in the newspapers in your market range. In recent years it has become common for the family to request charitable donations in lieu of flowers. However, family members still purchase flowers for the funeral, and many close friends and relatives still choose to send flowers.

It used to be that the family would be ordering funeral flowers before the death notice made it to the paper, but these days the internet has changed all that. By keeping tabs on the obits, you can express sympathy, mention that you saw the obituary, and even say something more personal ("He sounded like a nice man." "She was so young.") if a family member comes in or calls to order flowers. You don't have to get carried away. Don't dwell on the sadness and make your customers cry, but do make them realize they are dealing with a human being who has compassion as well as a business side.

Beware!

Customers who come in to order flowers for family members' funerals will quite likely cry at some point. If your shop can at all accommodate it, have an area off to the side where you can sit and take the order so that they need not be self conscious about being emotional at the counter. Keep a box of tissues there, too; that is always a comforting sign that they aren't the only ones who have been emotional while ordering funeral flowers.

Special Attention

Like airline pilots often say in their concluding message just before landing, customers have a great number of choices when it comes to doing business. You need to make people want

Smart Tip

If you can't find a delivery location and have to stop at someone's house to ask directions, remember everything makes an impression on someone about your business. You may be frustrated with your difficulty finding the right house for your delivery. But remember a cranky driver with a vehicle sign identifying her business who interrupts someone at his home can lose a potential customer—as well as a few of her friends when she tells the story. Instead, do the opposite—present her with a flower when you ring the doorbell and always leave a business card, perhaps even with a discount coupon. You may find the house you are looking for and pick up a couple customers on the way. Use it as a marketing opportunity.

to do their floral business with you. You can do this by making them feel that they are important, which shouldn't be too hard—they are.

This doesn't mean that you need to spend hours on the phone with each caller, or that you need to bend the rules or make your own job difficult. But you do need to make sure customers realize that their business is important to you and you will do your utmost to create floral arrangements that are perfect for their needs.

In the Shop

Despite the financial responsibility of employees, you will probably quickly conclude that florist shops are probably best not being a one-person shop. It is too difficult to just get into being creative with an order and then have to stop and answer the phone or greet a customer. Getting an answering machine during common business hours does not instill much confidence in customers, whether existing or new. The same goes for a customer walking into a shop and wandering around alone for a few minutes before seeing any sign of life.

Phone Service

The telephone is a critical sales tool for the retail florist. A lot of your business will probably come in via the phone.

First, be friendly. This sounds like a no-brainer, but your tone when you answer the phone is so important. Make callers feel like you are happy with your work, that flowers cheer people up.

Let them control the beginning of the phone call. Once you have established a good rapport, you can start to lead the conversation. You want to get all the information you need but not be on the phone for 20 minutes on a simple bouquet order.

Keep order forms beside the phone, and start to fill one out as soon as you understand that the caller wants to place an order. Either print a dozen of these out at the

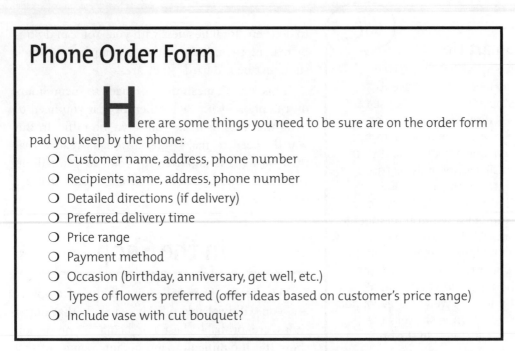

Phone Order Form

Here are some things you need to be sure are on the order form pad you keep by the phone:

- ○ Customer name, address, phone number
- ○ Recipients name, address, phone number
- ○ Detailed directions (if delivery)
- ○ Preferred delivery time
- ○ Price range
- ○ Payment method
- ○ Occasion (birthday, anniversary, get well, etc.)
- ○ Types of flowers preferred (offer ideas based on customer's price range)
- ○ Include vase with cut bouquet?

beginning of each day or have pads made up at your local quick printer. And tie a pen down near the phone—callers can get frustrated by being put on hold while you track down a pen. It seems like a small thing, but it makes it appear that you don't take many orders!

The Investigative Florist

When it comes to flowers, many customers don't know what they want. You will need to be a bit of a sleuth to gather information that will help you create that one-of-a-kind bouquet perfect for the recipient of the gift. Here are some questions to ask:

- *What is the occasion?* This of course is of first importance and the customer will probably tell you this without your asking. However, it will make a huge impact on everything else you ask and determines what direction you go in to fulfill the order. Funeral flowers are quite different from wedding flowers, and they are each a bit different from the flower arrangement for a new baby or new job.

- *What is the person like who is getting the flowers?* You are looking for things like "flamboyant," "bold," "chatty," "quiet"—anything that will tell you whether brightly colored tropical stems or more traditional flowers like daisies, roses, or sunflowers would be best.

- *What is the recipient's home like?* Is it a 200-year-old cape with exposed beams and wood floors or a contemporary condo with white carpets and white walls covered with Andy Warhol prints? This information can tell you a lot about the kind of arrangement that would be appropriate. A sweet bowl of daisies with a baby blue lace ribbon is going to be a little out of place in the condo.

- *If the arrangement isn't being sent to the person's home, ask about where it will be going.* Perhaps it is a get-well bouquet going to the hospital. If the person is in a semi-private room with little extra space, your 18-inch tall glass vase with large lilies is going to be an annoyance rather than a welcome sight. But if the person is

> **Tip...**
>
> **Smart Tip**
> While it seems obvious, answer the shop phone with the name of your business—"Good morning, Flo's Floral." Callers want to know they got the business they were calling before they launch into telling you what they want. Definitely say welcoming words—good morning, hello, good afternoon—and add your name if you want, but always always say your business name.

in a long-term stay in a private suite in the hospital, the large arrangement may be just the thing.

The key here is to ask as many questions as you need to get a feel for the recipient before you begin to talk about specific flowers and types of vases.

Once you have a sense of the type of arrangement, the topic of cost should come up. Simply ask the customer how much she wants to spend. This will then lead you to the next step.

Deliveries

If deliveries are going to be a significant portion of your business, which they almost have to be, then your location is going to be important. You will need a place to park a delivery vehicle with easy access to load from your shop. And you will need to be able to efficiently get to where you are headed without burning up a lot of time and gas driving miles before you get to the areas where most of your deliveries will take place.

It is best to call ahead to see if someone is going to be home to take delivery. Otherwise you will want to have preprinted notices that you can leave in the door to indicate that you have been there and to call with a time to deliver.

Don't feel like you always have to drop everything and head out the door with a delivery as soon as the arrangement is ready. These aren't pizzas. Be clear with customers about when they want the delivery; most will be fine with it occurring at any time on the appropriate day but always check to be sure. Try to group deliveries into similar areas of town or into one clump in the day if possible. Customers will understand that deliveries are made in a logical way as long as you are clear when they can expect delivery to occur.

Your Delivery Vehicle

One of the keys to successful delivery is a reliable vehicle. Successful delivery service is critical to good customer service in a florist business. Delivering your products leaves you with lots of things to consider.

> **Smart Tip** Tip...
>
> Get a GPS unit for your delivery vehicle. Load it with the mapping software appropriate to your delivery range. This simple tool will save you time, frustration, and ultimately money in the form of wasted gas. Learn to use the GPS unit to its maximum efficiency. And teach anyone who does deliveries how to use it, too.

What Kind of Vehicle?

Most florists use vans. If your business is large, you may want to invest in a box van or even a refrigerated vehicle, which means you can make more deliveries still using only one delivery employee (opposed to having multiple vans).

The vehicles that are targeted to younger consumers that want to pack their snowboards and other athletic equipment—Honda's Element or Toyota's Rav4—can be perfect for floral deliveries. Their cargo area is very resilient and washable, they typically are all-wheel drive (for deliveries in regions of the country where snow is an issue), and they tend to get great gas mileage. And as a bonus, their exteriors offer a lot of space for advertising.

It's best not to use your personal vehicle for deliveries if you can help it. For tax and insurance purposes, you would be wiser to have a vehicle specifically for your business. With a business that uses a vehicle a lot, this just makes sense.

Vehicle Maintenance Is Key

Be diligent about maintenance. Some things to keep in mind:

- *Change the oil per manufacturer recommendations.* Always have all of the fluids filled at the same time as the oil change, and check tire air pressure (including the spare), tire wear, belt wear, and windshield wiper status with each oil change.

- *Use a mechanic who is going to forewarn you about impending problems so you can have things fixed before they become an emergency.* It is best to avoid potential emergency situations whenever possible. The last thing you need is to waste time waiting for a tow and repair—with a vehicle filled with deliveries.
- *Although it is probably a good idea for anyone who uses the delivery vehicle to know how to change a tire and add oil; be sure to have either AAA membership or a towing binder on your insurance policy.* Keep all that information (as well as your vehicle insurance info) in the glove compartment. Be sure all drivers are named on your insurance policy and have their own AAA membership cards, because AAA is matched to the name not the vehicle.

When Things Go Wrong

Mistakes happen. The best thing to do is to confront mistakes head on. If you miss a delivery, call the customer and let him know. Don't just offer him his money back, that is already expected. Also offer something to make up for it—for example, a bigger bouquet, a discount on other orders. Usually customers will be understanding about one mistake.

If you find that a batch of flowers is sub-par, send a customer a note with a discount coupon. Acknowledging mistakes makes it clear you care about the quality of your work, are willing to make up for it, and want the customer to try you again for a better experience.

Irate customers who come into your store or call are best defused with honesty. The old adage "The customer is always right" comes in handy during these times. You will soon recognize the customer who is just going to complain every time about everything. There is nothing you can do about that. The best solution is to try to encourage those customers to do their business elsewhere.

Employee Training

Last, but not least, train your employees in customer service. Make it clear how you want them to greet customers, answer the phone, and deal with problems. How you behave is a good example for employees to follow, but it helps to lay out clear-cut customer service rules to follow.

A Single Stem
to a Whole
Garden

Your business can only grow so much by adding more customers to your existing operation. At some point, to gain more customers and more revenue from your existing customers, you also will need to expand what you offer. Some key questions to ask before you expand your business are:

- *What will your expansion cost in time?* This could be downtime for your current operation or the extra time it will require to operate the expanded business.

- *What will it cost in money?* Of course, there is always the initial cost of the expansion. But you also have to keep in mind that more product means you have to spend more money to acquire it. A larger store incurs more heating and cooling expense, more furnishings. And it all will probably mean adding an employee or two.

- *What will it bring the business in terms of increased revenue?*

- *What will it bring the business in terms of increased market?*

- *Do you really want to commit more to the business than you already do?* And more importantly, can you? There are only so many hours in a week no matter how you look at it.

Answering these questions may lead you to closing the door on expansion. Or it may leave you even that much more encouraged to expand. The main point is to think through all the details as carefully as you did in opening the shop in the first place.

Expanding Revenue, Not Customers

To gain more customers, you need to expand your market area. Sometimes that is not possible or desireable. So another approach is to expand what you offer your current customers to see if you can get them to buy more. It doesn't have to be in product. Are there additional services you could offer?

Wire Services

No floral business book would be complete without mentioning the floral wire services. There are several, but FTD and Teleflora capture most of the market. To be an affiliate of either of these, you typically need to apply, stock a certain quantity of certain flowers, meet a certain minimum of orders in a specified time period (or pay a penalty), and pay monthly dues. Most FTD and Teleflora business is done using a computer, with orders processed electronically.

There are specific arrangements that you create and specific pricing that you charge. The companies provide catalogs showing both. The downside can be that you put up the full cost of the flowers and supplies and are paid later. But they do offer additional revenue that you probably wouldn't get later.

While it sounds a tad complicated, it is probably more important to be a member of one or both of these than not—unless your shop is in an extremely rural area and you just would not have the volume.

Products

The simplest way to add revenue from existing customers is to have more in your shop for them to purchase. Look for new and unique lines that fit your shop's style. Find things that you enjoy. One of the nicest compliments you can get is when someone walks in your store and exclaims how unique your offering is. Stock greeting cards that have dried flowers on them. Or stock dried flowers. Add a section of candles and locally made candleholders, or T-shirts with hand painted flowers on them. Reserve wall space and encourage local artists to display their art in your shop; rotate the display monthly and take a commission on sales. If you are going to add more product, have fun with it.

Services

Perhaps there is a market in your area for a plant care service. Large offices or hotels often have a service that does the live decorating and services the plants once a week, watering, deadheading, taking care of pests and other problems, and replacing plants with fresh ones.

If you have the expertise (or the market can bear you hiring someone who does), you could extend the same kind of service to landscaping. Hotels, office buildings, malls and other retail establishments are all potential customers for this kind of service.

Classes

Kitchen and food stores do it all the time—offer cooking classes to their customer base. Can you offer classes? Although doing it at your store is best, if your shop doesn't have the space, you can often find inexpensive, even free, spaces around the community to conduct your classes. Flower arranging classes can be a great way to expand the amount of revenue from each customer—once they become hooked on arranging, they can buy their supplies from you. To give them an incentive to do so, offer a discount to anyone who has gone through one of your classes.

> **Fun Fact**
>
> If you are looking for a busman's holiday, Lompoc Valley near Santa Barbara, California, is the self-proclaimed "flower capital of the world." The city of Lompoc's nickname is "The City of Arts and Flowers."

Wider Market

Another revenue expansion is to simply increase the market area to which you deliver. Carefully research the florists in these other markets because the market could well be already tapped. You would have to increase your revenue enough to afford either an extra delivery vehicle, more cost for your current delivery service, or more trips a day using your current delivery vehicle. It can be worth it but has to be planned.

New Niches

As we have discussed in previous chapters, it is important for a floral shop to find a niche and become known as an expert in that area. Weddings are the main one—and there seem to be plenty of weddings to go around.

But once you have that niche well under control, are there other niches you might explore? Have you gotten involved with the funeral homes in your area or even cemetery flowers? Perhaps you could contact the local memorials business and offer to provide them with small arrangements that they could place as an added touch when they install a memorial—how nice for the family to come see a new gravestone and find a lovely arrangement there as well.

Thinking outside of the box is critical in standing out in the retail industry.

Physical Expansion

In order to take your revenue to the next level, you may need to seriously consider expanding the physical space of your shop. Chances are that isn't possible if you stay in your current location, but keep your ears open for that possibility—for example, a shop on one side of you closing.

Your expansion can house more of the same thing you are selling now. You can also choose to focus the expansion area on new lines of products. Or you can make a space conducive to meetings and classes and offer those services.

You may just need more space to make the shop work a little more efficiently. This is important, but be careful. First, look for ways to make your shop more efficient in the space you have. When you incur expenses (both the initial cost of expansion and the ongoing increase in overhead), it should be able to not only pay for itself but also bring in more revenue.

Additional Sites

If you think your current market is tapped, and you would rather not expand in your current retail shop, consider adding a branch in a new market. Scout out areas in the 50 to 60 mile range that could be targets for a new flower shop. Or investigate

Bright Idea

A new branch of your existing store is a great way for a small business to offer a promotion to an employee. Give one the chance to run the "old" shop so you can focus on getting the new branch up and running.

whether there are any shops for sale that you could buy to use as a branch of your flagship store.

Provided you have developed strong branding for your current store, it shouldn't take long to establish your brand in the new market. Remember the importance of consistent signage (not just name but also style) and marketing materials. However, if your expansion store is in a very different market—perhaps more working class than the upscale clientele of your existing store—don't force a square peg in a round hole. The new store needs to stay true to its market.

Don't feel like your branch store needs to be a stone's throw from your current store, but also don't open up the new shop so far away that you are on the road as much as you are in either shop. You will need to plan to be in the new store quite a bit in the first year of its existence.

New Businesses

There are many avenues in which to get into the floral business. Your own interests and personality will lead you down one path or the other. Some are geared toward those who like to spend a lot of time outside; others, like the wholesale business, may mean you spend a lot of time behind a desk on the phone.

Garden Center

Does being outside compared to being in the retail shop setting appeal to you? A full-fledged garden center might be just the ticket. The garden center offers live plants, including houseplants, annuals and perennials for planting, vegetable plants for the summer garden, and even small trees.

Because of this huge range of product, the revenue possibilities are much greater than a small retail florist. On the other hand, the inventory needs and start-up costs are much greater as well. If you are going to offer flower and vegetable plants for the gardener to plant, you will need a greenhouse where you can start seeds ahead of time to be ready for planting at the start of the season.

You will need a lot of sidelines like fertilizers, pesticides, seeds, and potting soil. And you will probably want to have an array of garden furnishings such as stepping stones, arbors, and benches.

However, if you are looking for a way to expand your florist shop, you can combine the two. Find a location where you can have your florist shop on the same site as the garden center.

Don't forget, in many areas of the country, garden centers are seasonal. This can be nice—you have an automatic few months of the year when you can kick back a little, maybe even take a trip to unwind and prepare yourself for the next busy season. But if you keep your florist shop, you may find you have no down time at all.

Landscaping Business

Landscaping businesses are often associated with garden centers. This allows the landscaping business to purchase the products they need at wholesale prices. Landscapers usually focus on businesses or homes. Typically, the business owner or homeowner will sign a contract for regular service. You can just design and install new landscaping, but it is best if you can also get a service contract to make sure the landscaping continues to reflect your good work.

Wholesale Floral

Wholesale floral businesses were discussed in other chapters, but the topic bears further discussion. You may find in the course of your career as a florist that the wholesale side of things intrigues you enough that you would like to get into it. Because it is so international and involves lots of import business, wholesaling can be exciting. However, for Mary B. of Wyoming Florists, it provides little attraction: "I've always been interested only in the retail side; it is the most creative. Wholesaling seems to involve just passing the product through." You can combine wholesale and retail, but they are really be two separate, and very different, businesses.

> ### Bright Idea
> Even if you are not 100 percent sure adding another branch is the way you want to expand, have a business broker keep you apprised of any existing florists that come up for sale. You never know, the right situation may make it a very appealing approach to expansion.

Appendix
Florist Business Resources

They say you can never be too rich or too thin. While those points could be argued, we believe you can never have too many resources. Therefore, we present for your consideration a wealth of sources for you to check into, check out, and harness for your own personal information blitz.

These sources are tidbits, ideas to get you started on your research. They are by no means the only sources out there, and they should not be taken as the Ultimate Answer. We have done our research, but businesses tend to move, change, fold, and expand. As we have repeatedly stressed, do your homework. Get out and start investigating.

As an additional tidbit to get you going, I strongly support the following: If you haven't yet joined the internet age, do it! Surfing the net is like waltzing through a library, with a breathtaking array of resources literally at your fingertips.

Associations

American Floral Industry Association
P.O. Box 420244
Dallas, TX 75342
(214) 742-2747
www.afia.net

American Floral Endowment
P.O. Box 945
Edwardsville, IL 62025
(618) 692-0045
www.endowment.org

American Institute of Floral Designers
721 Light Street
Baltimore, MD 21230
(301) 752-3318
www.aifd.org

Association of Floriculture Professionals
2130 Stella Court
Columbus, OH 43215
(614) 487-1117
www.ofa.org

American Orchid Society
16700 AOS Lane
Delray Beach, FL 33446
(561) 404-2000
www.orchidweb.org

Association of Specialty Cut Flower Growers
MPO Box 268
17½ W. College Street
Oberlin, OH, 44074
(440) 774-2887
www.ascfg.org

Flower Promotion Organization
(952) 545-7943 (Executive Director)
www.flowerpossibilities.org

Fresh Produce and Floral Council
16700 Valley View Avenue,
Suite 130
La Mirada, CA 90638
(714) 739-0177
www.fpfc.org

Produce Marketing Association
1500 Casho Mill Road
P.O. Box 6036

Newark, DE 19714
(302) 738-7100
www.pma.org

Society of American Florists
1601 Duke Street
Alexandria, VA 22314
(800) 336-4743
www.aboutflowers.com

Wholesale Florist and Florist Supply Association
147 Old Solomons Island Road, Suite 302
Annapolis, MD 21401
(410) 573-0400
www.wffsa.org

Trade Magazines

Florist's Review Magazine
Florists' Review Enterprises
P.O. Box 4368
Topeka, KS 66604
(785) 266-0888
Monthly guide to operating a successful florist business.

Super Floral Retailing
Florists' Review Enterprises
P.O. Box 4368
Topeka, KS 66604
(785) 266-0888
Monthly guide for supermarket, mass market, and high-volume florists.

Walk-In Cooler Manufacturers

American Panel Corporation
5800 S.E. 78th Street
Ocala, FL 34472-3412
(352) 245-7055

Snowhite Coolers
(305) 836-5540
www.snowhitecoolers.com

Bush Refrigeration
(800) 220-2874
www.bushrefrigeration.com

State Floral Associations

Alabama State Florists Association
2798 John Hawkins Parkway, Ste 124
Hoover, AL 35244
(205) 989-8001

Alaska State Florists Association
253 Idaho Street
Anchorage, AK 95044
(907) 333-6908

Arizona State Florists Association
850 East Camino Alberca
Tucson, AZ 85718
(520) 742-1409
www.azstateflorists.org

Arkansas State Florists Association
P.O. Box 500
Plumerville, AR 72127
(501) 354-1160

Ozark Florists Association
1111 Garrison
Fort Smith, AR 72901
(479) 783-5146

California State Florists Association
1521 I Street
Sacramento, CA 95814
(916) 448-5266

Colorado Greenhouse Growers Association
Wholesale Florists of Colorado
7475 Dakin Street, Ste 540
Denver, CO 80221-6919
(303) 427-8132
www.cgga.org

Connecticut Florists Association
590 Main St. Bart Center
Monroe, CT 06468
(203) 268-9000

Florida State Florists Association
1612 South Dixie Highway
Lake Worth, FL 33460
(561) 585-9491

Georgia State Florists Association
789 Roswell Street
Marietta, GA 30060
(912) 524-2386

Idaho State Florists Association
715 North Main Street
Pocatello, ID 83204
(208) 232-5476

Illinois State Florists Association
1231 North LaSalle
Ottowa, IL 61350
(800) 416-4732
www.illinoisflorists.org

Indiana State Florists Association
P.O. Box 133
Monrovia, IN 46157
(317) 996-2241

Society of Iowa Florists and Growers
48428 290th Avenue
Rolfe, IA 50581
(712) 848-3251

Kansas State Florists Association
112 South Main Street
Greensburg, KS 67054
(620) 723-2603

Kentucky Florists Association
3954 Cane Run Road
Louisville, KY 40211
(502) 778-1666

Louisiana State Florists Association
224 Hodges Road
Ruston, LA 71270
(318) 255-2671

Maine State Florists Association
216-A Maine Street
Brunswick, ME 04011
(207) 729-8895

Michigan Floral Association
P.O. Box 67
Haslett, MI 48840
(517) 575-0110
www.michiganfloral.org

Minnesota State Florists Association
1536 Woodland Drive
Woodbury, MN 55125
(952) 934-4505

Mississippi State Florists Association
403 Highway 11 North
Ellisville, MS 39437
(601) 477-8381

Montana State Florists Association
P.O. Box 1456
Great Falls, MT 59403
(406) 452-6489

Nebraska Florists Society
1900 SW 22nd Street
Lincoln, NE 68522
(402) 421-2613

North Nevada Florists Association
519 Ralston Streeet
Reno, NV 89503
(775) 323-8951

New Hampshire Florists Association
21 Roger Road
Goffstown, NH 03045
(603) 627-8828

New Jersey State Florists Association
88 Fawnridge Drive
Long Valley, NJ 07853
(908) 876-1850

New Mexico State Florists Association
P.O. Box 3342
Roswell, NM 88202
(505) 265-1019

New York Florists Association
249 East 149th Street
Bronx, NY 10451
(718) 585-3060

North Carolina State Florists Association
P.O. Box 41368
Raleigh, NC 27629
(919) 876-0687

Ohio Florists Association
2130 Stella Court #200
Columbus, OH 43215
(614) 487-1117
www.ofa.org

Oklahoma State Florists Association
P.O. Box 614
Drumright, OK 74030
(918) 352-3906

Pennsylvania Floral Industry Association
1924 North Second Street
Harrisburg, PA 17102
(717) 238-0758

Rhode Island Retail Florists Association
820 Boston Neck Road
North Kingstown, RI 02852
(401) 294-9015

South Carolina Florists Association
1663 Russell Street NE
Orangeburg, SC 29115
(803) 534-3780

Tennessee State Florists Association
P.O. Box 240235
Memphis, TN 38124
(901) 323-4521

Texas State Florists Association
P.O. Box 140255
Austin, TX 78714
(512) 834-0361
www.tsfa.org

Central Virginia Florists Association
501 Courthouse Road
Richmond, VA 23236
(804) 378-0700

Washington Florists Association
P.O. Box 1591
Edmond, WA 98020
www.pspf.org

Wisconsin Florists Association
P.O. Box 483
Menomonee Falls, WI 53052
(262) 251-6010

Glossary

Cut flowers: Flowers that are sold by the stem, opposed to live flowers sold as plants.

Farmer's market: An open-air market that is a good place to sell flowers.

Florist: A person who sells flowers.

Focus group: A marketing tool that uses a gathering of people representative of your customer base from whom you get feedback about products and services.

GPS: Short for "Global Positioning System."

Greenhouse: A plant-selling operation where many of the plants are grown and sold live.

Guard petals: An outer, protective layer of petals on a rose bud.

Hydration: Getting cut flowers back to the moisture status they need.

Ikebana: The Japanese art of flower arranging.

Impulse items: Things for sale in a retail store that are not part of the customer's planned purchases. There items are often found near the cash-out area.

Independent contractors: People you hire who work for themselves.

Niche: Your shop's specialty, e.g., weddings or landscaping.

Nursery: Similar to a greenhouse only the focus is almost exclusively on growing plants and trees from seeds and seedlings to the stage where they can be sold. Many operations mix a nursery, greenhouse, and florist shop on the same premises.

Pick-your-own: Customers come to your farm/garden and cut their own flowers.

Reach-in: The cooler on the sales floor of a florist shop that customers can reach in to and pick out their own arrangements or pick the flowers they want arranged; also used for cut flower storage.

Service contract: A legal agreement for providing services such as landscaping or weekly plant care.

Sidelines: All of the extras in your shop that aren't specifically related to flowers, such as greeting cards or wind chimes.

Spoilage: The term used for the inventory that goes bad before it gets used; this term is common to any business that deals in perishable inventory.

Stock rotation: The phrase referring to using up your oldest inventory first—you keep rotating your older flowers to the front to use up first.

Storefront: The area of your store that is visible from the street by passersby either walking or driving.

Undercapitalization: Not starting your business with an adequate amount of capital to keep it running until the business begins to generate revenue and profit.

Walk-in: This phrase can have two meanings: 1) A refrigeration unit that is of a large enough size that a person can walk into it; this is typically in the back area of a florist shop and is for storing large amounts of flowers. 2) The business a retail store gets that walks in the door, opposed to calling first and ordering by phone/email/internet.

Index